A STEP BY STEP GUID
T
EVERYTHING
YOU NEED TO KNOW
ABOUT BEING A GUITAR PLAYER!

by John A. MacLachlan

The Beginners Series

For Keyboards, Guitar, Drums, Bass Guitar & Saxophone.

Written by John during the late spring of 1997. All music examples specially composed for the project.

Edited by: Clive Gregory

Assistant editor: G. Ellwood

Photographs by Michael Pearse

Artwork and design by Clive Gregory

Text and music typeset by R & C Gregory Publishing Limited

Imaging by Pulse Graphics Ltd, Kent, England.

Special thanks to: Rubiah Gregory, Peter Wall, Michael Pearse, Graham Mitchell, Ben Cooper, Mike Riley and Dan at Pulse and all at Colourscope, without whom this series of books would never have been possible.

First Edition published 1997

Published by
R & C Gregory Publishing Limited
Suite 7, Unit 6, Beckenham Business Centre, Cricket Lane, Kent. BR3 1LB.

R. & C. gregory
PUBLISHING LIMITED

ISBN 1 901690 11 3

Printed by CS PRINT & DISPLAY Limited, Croydon, England.

This book is dedicated to my mum Ann, also Jim and Andy. To Criena, my partner and mother of my musical daughter Alexandra. In addition, special thanks to my tutors, especially Peter Driver at Goldsmiths College, London.

Also to a very special person, Margaret Hubicki F.R.A.M., O.B.E.

John MacLachlan's road to teaching has been one of thorough study and grounding, firstly classical guitar at the Kent Music School, moving onto studying jazz and contemporary music at Goldsmiths College in London. A teacher with over ten years experience John is one of the most dedicated music educators in the country. His battle against dyslexia has been a motivating rather than negative force in his musical life and he is renowned for his work teaching people with dyslexia and other learning difficulties.

His experience in helping such a large number of students overcome severe learning problems has lead to a book that is easy for anyone to follow - making music is the priority regardless of ambition or talent. The early examples in this book will enable students to create music almost as soon as the guitar is out of its box.

CONTENTS

INTRODUCTION

Welcome to the world of Guitar and Music. Good luck with this book and hope it helps.

This book is designed for total beginners to get you started on the road to good guitar playing. Playing the guitar well has as much to do with having the right attitude and understanding your role as a guitarist, as it has to do with practising or rehearsing with a band.

The Guitar is just about the most popular instrument in the world today, thanks to rock guitarists like; Peter Green, Eric Clapton, Jimi Hendrix, Jimmy Page, Gary Moore etc., and so many more in Classical, Jazz and other forms of popular music. However, we now have to put it together ourselves

As well as showing you the basics of technique and helping you to understand how music is put together, this book will try and ensure that when you're good enough to be in a band you understand the musicians around you. There are even tips on how to perform live, how to handle the pressure of the studio etc.

This book is specifically intended to be easy to use, to enable you to quickly get on with the business of playing guitar.

So what do you need to know to become a good guitarist?

1. Technique: The mechanics of finger movement. This book will outline what is important and useful in developing technique and will give you a few great exercises that will develop your hands and last a lifetime.

2. Musicianship: You need to become a musician and need to understand how music is put together to function as a useful (and therefore, popular) guitarist.

3. Composition and Improvisation: Most guitarists prefer to write their own parts - this book will outline how this is done. All good guitarists play with freedom. This means that they react to other musicians and even the audience in the way they play and deliver their parts. This varies from subtle adjustments to their regular part, to full-blown improvisation, where there is very little in the guitar part that is pre-composed.

4. Working with others: This book will try and give you some idea about the musicians you will work with. Also there will be tips about how to cope with live and studio playing - what others will expect of you.

5. Understanding the role of the Guitarist; probably the best thing that you can get from this book is to really understand what it is to be a guitarist.

Your First Time
Getting To Know Your Guitar

Well, you've done it. After months of saving, you've finally walked into that shop and, instead of annoying the proprietor with yet another request to try out the guitar of your dreams, you just pulled out that wallet and counted out your hard-earned.

Now you've got it home - the anticipation is almost too much - suddenly you panic!

"What do I *do* with it"? Is it still going to be in tune after that minor collision with the bus on the way home?

And there's worse...

HOW THE HELL DO I PLAY IT?

Don't worry, you've invested in the best book in the world for beginners. Let's get aquainted with the hardware!

The bridge and tailpiece assembly. Best for sustain when made of brass. Ideally each string should have its own 'saddle' so that it can be presicely positioned. The tailpiece really is there to hold the end of the string. Sometimes the strings need to be fed through holes in the guitar from the back. Also, on some guitars, the tailpiece contains the tremelo unit.

The tuning pegs are actually called machine heads. They are either arranged (as in this diagram) along one side of the headstock or there will be 3 on each side - neither is better or worse - just a matter of styling.

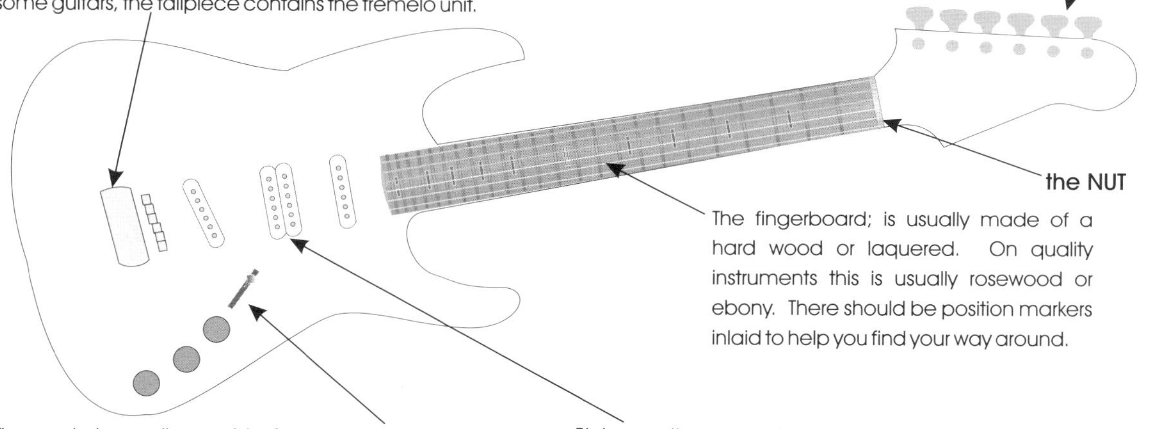

The fingerboard; is usually made of a hard wood or laquered. On quality instruments this is usually rosewood or ebony. There should be position markers inlaid to help you find your way around.

The controls usually consist of a pickup selector switch. This is usually a lever type but can be rotary. If there are three control knobs then the first two are usually volume for each pick-up and the furthest one is a general tone control. On cheaper guitars and vintage guitars the tone controls will be simple filter devices filtering out high frequencies, giving the effect of high treble (no filter) at one end and bass (full filter) at the other. Many guitars have powered (by battery) circuits enabling much more sophisticated tone circuitry. There are so many variations to this that if you buy one, make sure there's a manual to help you understand how it works. Do make sure that these circuits are quiet - cheap ones hiss - not good. Whatever the circuit, you will put in hours experimenting trying to find your sound - there's no short cut to this but even if there was, it would be no fun!

Pick-ups; there are two main types; Humbucker and single coil. Humbuckers were originally designed to eliminate hum and are basically two pick-ups laid side by side. As the current flows in different directions in each pick-up the hum that is naturally generated is cancelled. In practise these pick-ups are associated with warm, beefy sounds. Single coil are more effective for jangly tones. The generalised example shows two single coil pick-ups either side of a humbucker. This arrangement is now quite common and gives a huge array of different tones.

tuning the guitar

Firstly, if you have just bought your guitar with this book ask the shop to tune it before you leave and try and get it home without knocking it. Take care when learning to tune - even if you've bought a tuner. Turn the machine heads (tuning pegs) slowly and progressively - always listen to the pitch of the note change when you turn. There are many aids to tuning:

1. Pitch Pipes; simply blow through each pipe and tune each string to the pitch of the pipes.

2. Electronic tuners; when you play a string, the tuner picks up the vibration and the needle or lights tell us when we are lower or higher than the note. (Watch the calibration of each tuner as they can vary - important to know if you're working with other musicians each with their own tuner.)

3. Tuning fork; this is a good, inexpensive tuning device and one you can carry around.

To tune the guitar by ear, you need a reference note to start with. If you have a piano, play the note marked in fig. 1. This will correspond to the low E string on the guitar. If not, you will need a tuning fork or pitch pipes. A tuning fork will sound one note only, this will be marked on the fork. Tune the string with the same name/note as this first.

When you have your low E string (or whichever string that corresponds to your tuning fork) in tune with the reference note, fret the low E string at the 5th fret. This 'new' note should be the same as the next string played open. See fig. 4, the arrows show you which note to fret to match the next string played open. Watch out for the B string!

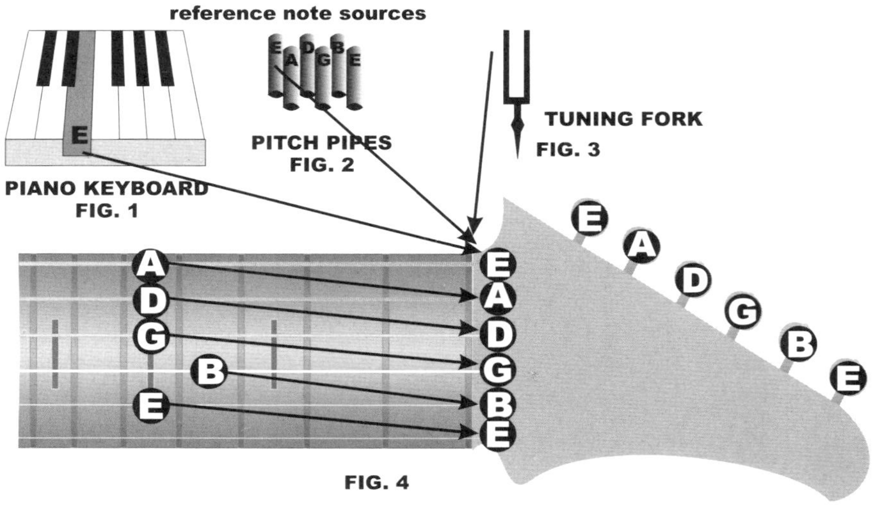

Even if you decide to buy an electronic tuner and even if this is really high quality and expensive, learn to use your ears when tuning. Obviously, if you use pitch pipes or a tuning fork you will need to use your ears to tune.

There is more on ear training on page 29, for now, try and really learn the sound that is made when you play two strings that are next to each other. Listen to each string individually, try humming or singing the note of the first string, then the next string. The difference or distance between two notes in music is called an interval. The interval between two adjacent strings is called a 'perfect fourth'. (The interval from the G string to the B string is a different sound, called a major 3rd.) This name you can find out more about later but the sound you can learn - practise singing the 'tune' created by two open strings played one after the other. There are not many tunes that begin with this sound but there are two quite famous ones; Wagner's 'Bridal March' and 'Apache' by The Shadows.

As well as trying to learn this sound it is also possible to learn the sound of one note such as your low E string - without reference to anything else. This will take time to acquire but if you keep singing and listening, you'll surprise yourself oneday when you tune without any tuning aid or reference note.

practising

You should find your own space and time every day. If you're a total beginner, 30 minutes is plenty. As you get more used to playing, try 45 minutes. After a while, if you can stay focused and you're enjoying yourself, practise as long as you like. Just be aware of your highs and lows. However, it is regular practise that gives results.

If in doubt, a little and often!

Make sure there is no-one around to cause your practise time to turn into a performance, this is a different thing... Coming soon!

posture

sitting

When sitting, adjust the strap so that you just feel the weight of the guitar on your neck, even though your right leg is supporting the body under the cutaway. With acoustic guitars there is no need to use the strap, although you will position the right arm on the body of the guitar more heavily than you would with the electric.

standing

The strap should be a little bit longer - though not too much longer. And your nose should be roughly in line with the 12th fret.

technique

The way you hold your guitar and the way you press down the strings with your left hand and pick with your right is going to affect your ability as a guitar player for ever. Having a good technique will enable you to do more as a musician and guitar player. Effort now, will be paid back a hundred times in the future.

left hand technique

Bring your left hand up from your side. Don't twist the arm, just raise naturally from the elbow.

Begin by placing the thumb roughly under the sixth fret, in the centre of the back of the neck (see fig. 1 & 2). Then place your index finger (known as 1st finger) between the fourth and fifth frets nearly touching the fifth fret on one of the middle strings. Allow the wrist to bend gently so that you can maintain your thumb position. Next, position your middle finger (2nd finger) nearly touching the 6th fret; your ring finger (3rd finger) nearly touching the 7th fret; and your little finger (4th finger) nearly touching the 8th fret (see fig. 3).

Try and practise positioning your hand and fingers on each string in turn, getting used to spacing your fingers and curving your wrist.

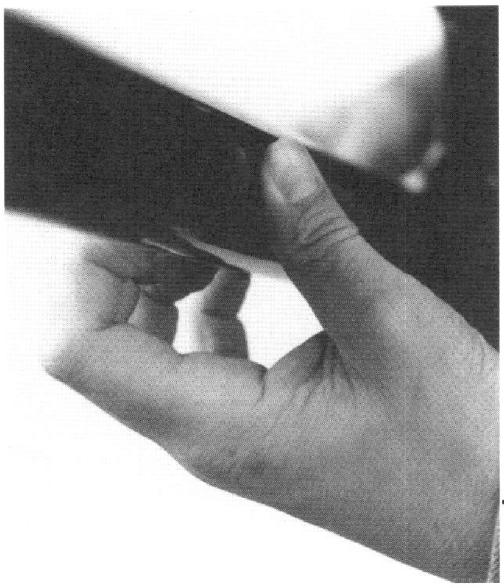

fig. 1

fig. 3

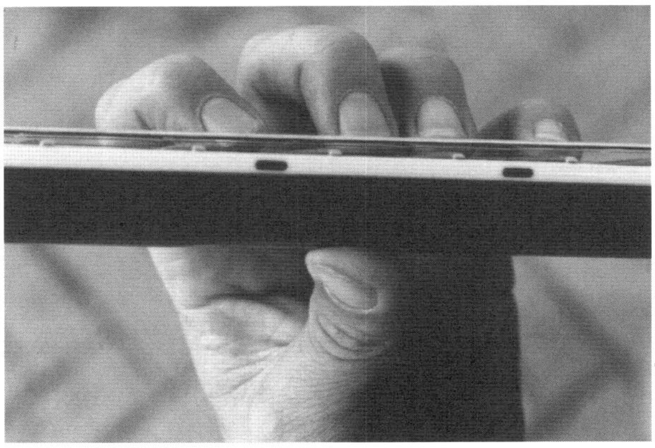

fig. 2

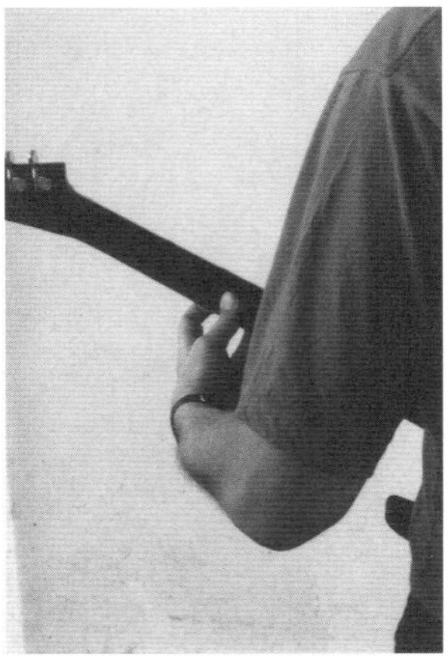

fig. 4

right hand technique

For the purposes of this book I'm going to concentrate only on pick (or plectrum) technique. There are, of course, some great guitarists, including many electric guitarists that use the fingers of the right hand to pluck the strings. However, whilst you should feel free to experiment with this, it is generally for more advanced playing.

There are many types of pick. Their thickness (measured in millimetres) has the greatest effect on right hand technique and sound but both are also affected by the type of material the pick is made from. Usually they are made of nylon or hard plastic, but some players use old sixpences (like a 5p if you're under 30) and anything else they can lay their hands on. If it feels good and gives a good sound - give it a try.

Generally, you are unlikely to break the bank by choosing five or six different types and experimenting with them all. You'll soon find one stands out as being your kind of pick.

Your grip on the pick should be firm but not too hard. Try and ensure that there is not too much showing from underneath the thumb and index finger.

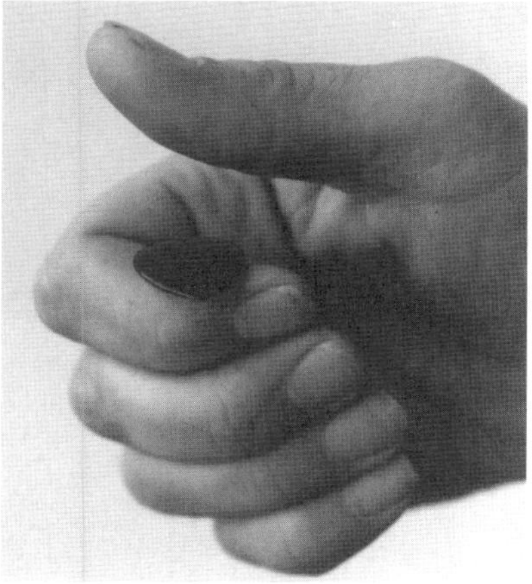

getting a grip on the pick

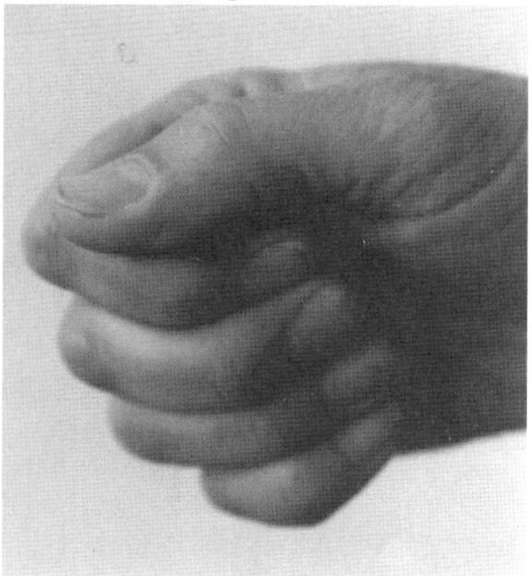

Always remember that the movement comes from the wrist, not the elbow. Even later when strumming, most of the movement is in the wrist, even though that movement is wider.

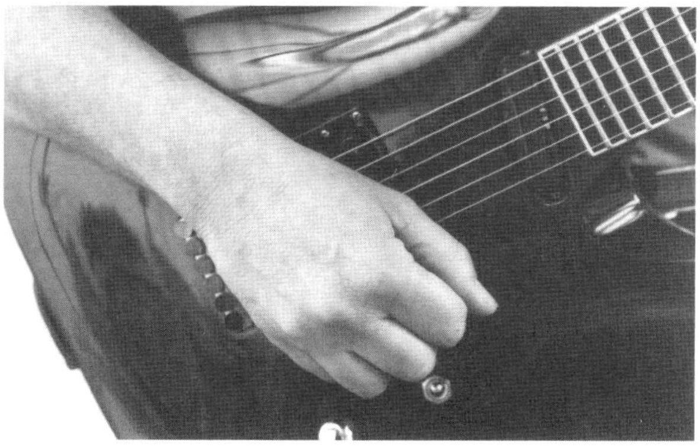

understanding the notation and examples

In this book I use several forms of notation. The best way to convey information about music is through the use of standard music notation and chord symbols. Your goal should be to only need these standard forms of notation by the end of this book. However, it's not my intention to force you to read music and it does take some getting used to, although I must stress that it is not difficult. So, in addition to standard music notation I am using guitar neck graphics, chord graphics, tablature (tab) and in some cases photographs, for greater clarity. Compare all the forms and work towards a full understanding of correct music notation - you know it makes sense.

the guitar neck graphic

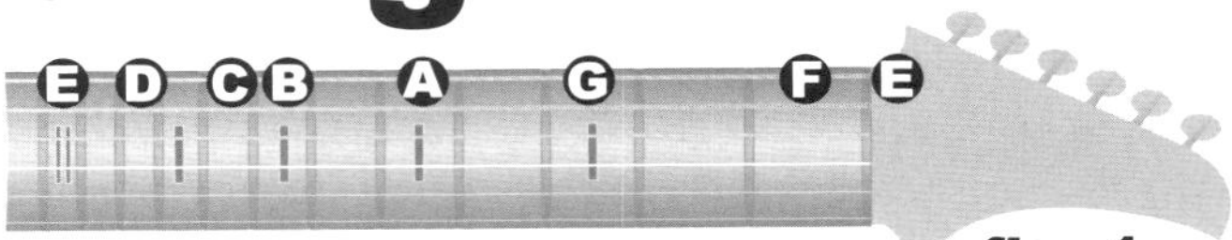

fig. 1

The guitar neck graphic allows you to see at a glance where the relevant notes are on the neck.

This graphic will often be used in pairs - one to show the note names and their positions on the neck - the other to show in which order to play these notes.

So remember, the numbers represent the order in which you play the notes, unless otherwise stated.

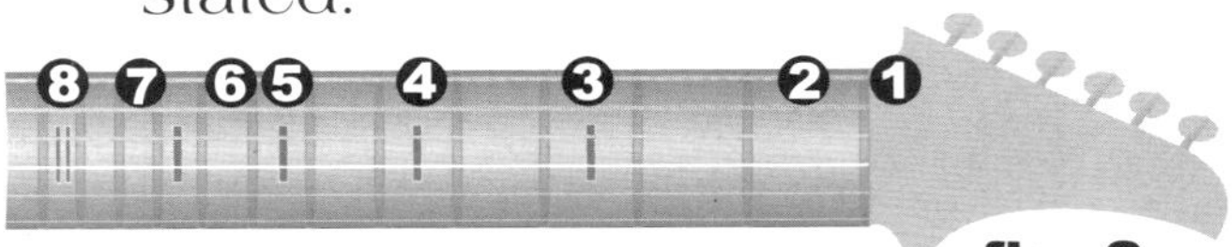

fig. 2

the chord graphic

fig. 3

As with the guitar neck graphic, the chord graphic makes it really easy to see which notes to play and where on the neck to play them.

Again, either note names or numbers can be used but unlike the guitar neck graphic, which is used to represent melody, the chord graphic is showing you which notes you play AT THE SAME TIME.

fig. 4

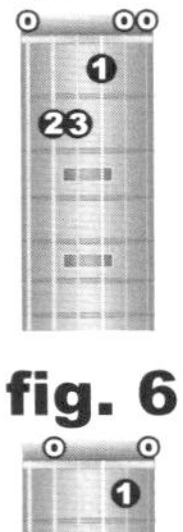

=

fig. 5

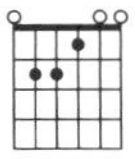

fig. 6

=

fig. 7

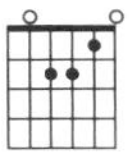

So, in this case, numbers can be used to represent which finger(s) plays the note.

These graphics are based on the conventional chord graphic (see fig. 5 & 7). The hope is that the graphics used in this book will make learning melody and chords very 'visual' and therefore, easier to begin with.

tab

TAB uses six lines drawn across the page. Each line represents a string on the guitar. The low E string (thickest string - 6th string) is at the bottom (sometimes this line is thicker) and the high E string (thinnest - 1st string) is at the top.

Numbers can be placed on each line or string - these numbers are FRET NUMBERS and tell you which fret to position your finger behind.

If tab accompanies standard music notation (usual) then it rarely contains rhythm information (this is found in the music notation part) - but rhythm information is usually included if tab is on its own. Rhythm notation is the same in tab as standard music notation.

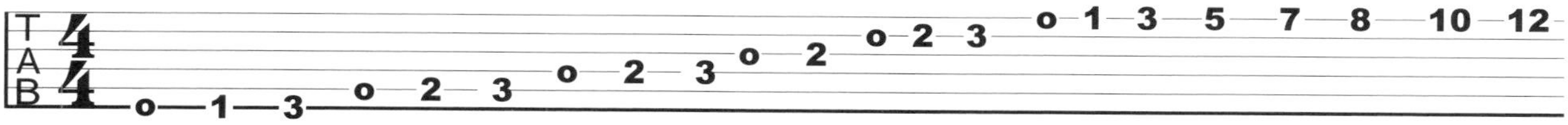

music notation

Standard music notation is perceived as difficult by non-musicians. Understanding written music and learning guitar lines etc. is actually quite easy. Reading at sight - immediately playing a piece of music that you've never seen before does require serious study, but need not concern you unless you want to work professionally.

There are five lines drawn across the page. Unlike tab these lines have nothing to do with the strings of a guitar or bass. They are simply a 'grid', called a STAFF (plural - Stave). When we look at a staff we see lines and spaces. Both lines and spaces are used to indicate the pitch (name) of a note.

In order to 'activate' a staff a 'clef' is needed. There are different types of clef but as guitar players we only need learn the Treble Clef - 𝄞.
This symbol is also known as the 'G' Clef, as it positions where the note 'G' is placed on the 'grid' or staff.

Once the clef is in place, all other notes take up their relative positions. Each line or space represents a different letter of the alphabet. So the space above the 'G' line, marked by the clef, is the note 'A', and the space below the 'G' line is 'F'.

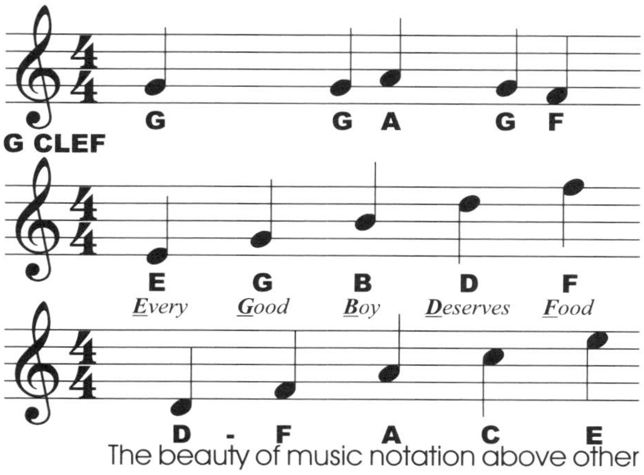

The beauty of music notation above other alternatives is, that once you're over the basics, you can look at the music and imagine the sound, long before your ear has been trained to do this with 100% accuracy. You can see the melody rise and fall and it is easy to see whether the rhythm is simple or busy, on the beat or heavily syncopated (off the beat).

Rhythm notation is dealt with on page 19.

pick basics

Practise plucking (one string at a time) using both down and up strokes. Allow the pick to 'flow' through the string, simply feel the movement from the wrist and practise making this feel the most natural thing in the world.

Practise playing the pick in the following ways:

1. all down strokes
2. all up strokes
3. down up, down up
4. up down, up down.

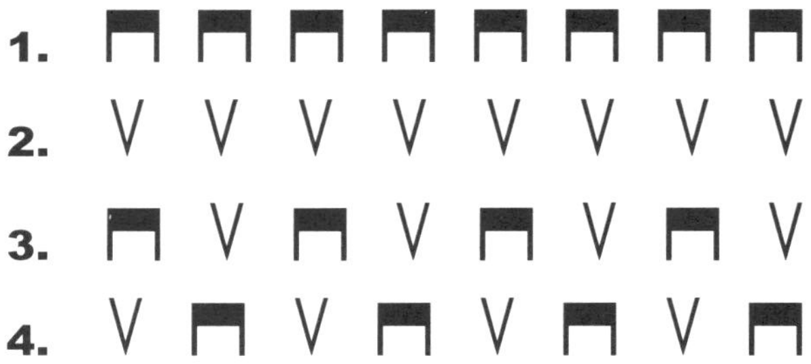

sign for downstroke

sign for upstroke

both hands - working together

Co-ordinating both hands precisely takes time for anybody to achieve. Your biggest enemy to good co-ordination is impatience. Start by practising everything slowly. During the following exercises and in all your early practise sessions, remain patient and concentrate on listening and looking. Listen carefully to every note you play. Is the left hand finger in position when the right hand plucks with the pick? or do you get a kind of glitch in the sound, where there is no pitch to start with? or an open string sound followed by the correct note? This means your left hand is arriving later than the right hand plucking the string. If the note is unexpectedly short, then you are releasing the left hand finger too early.

In a perfect world, both the left hand finger finds its note at the same time as the right hand plucks - this would be perfect co-ordination. In reality, the left hand usually is best anticipating notes in advance, ensuring that they are ready when the right hand plucks.

The left hand fingers have to deal with two states.

1. Putting fingers down
2. Releasing fingers.

This is fairly obvious. One surprise you may find is that releasing fingers is more difficult than putting fingers down. However, for now, get used to both states. Try to be aware of the problems that each creates for you.

Try the following group of exercises. Do these as pairs, firstly as exercises putting fingers down and secondly as exercises releasing fingers. Potentially, there a lot of exercises on this page. Don't attempt them all at first but as you improve, add more to your list.

EXERCISE 1: The following exercise uses only the 1st (index) and 2nd (middle) fingers of the left hand only. Although this could be played almost anywhere on the neck, starting at the fifth fret is very comfortable for the hand. Check pages 5 and 6 to ensure your technique is looking right and play the exercise very slowly. In this exercise you are practising putting fingers down onto the fingerboard. The right hand can take any approach from the previous page but it's easiest to start with all down strokes. When this is comfortable and you have a clean (nicely co-ordinated) sound, try another pick variation; all up strokes and, most important of all, down up, down

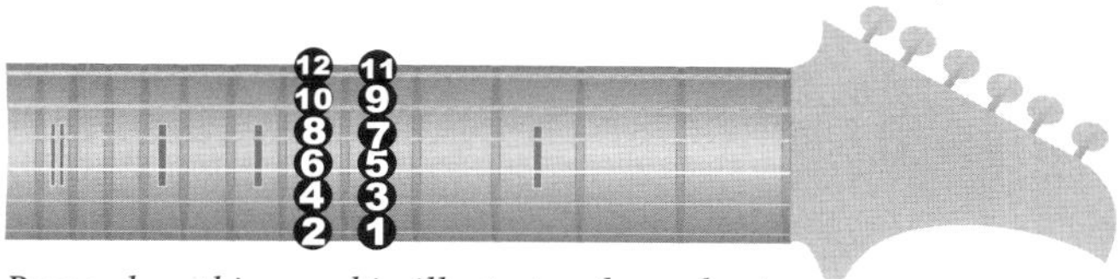

Remember, this graphic illustrates the order in which you play the notes

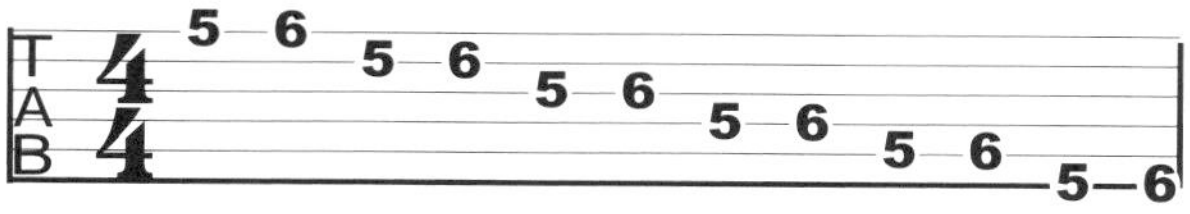

TAB is showing you which frets to play on (behind). The sequence of notes is from left to right.

EXERCISE 2: This exercise is the same as exercise 1, except that this time you play the 2nd finger followed by the first finger. In other words you are practising finger release. For most people this is more difficult to time and co-ordinate between the hands. Once again, just practise slowly at first making sure that the co-ordination between the right hand plucking the strings with the pick is precise with the left hand.

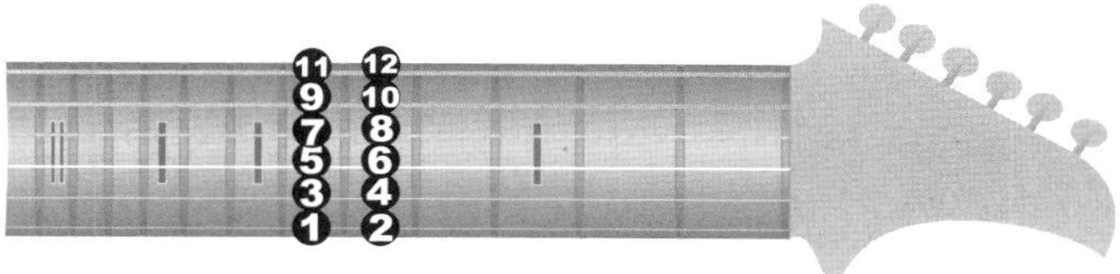

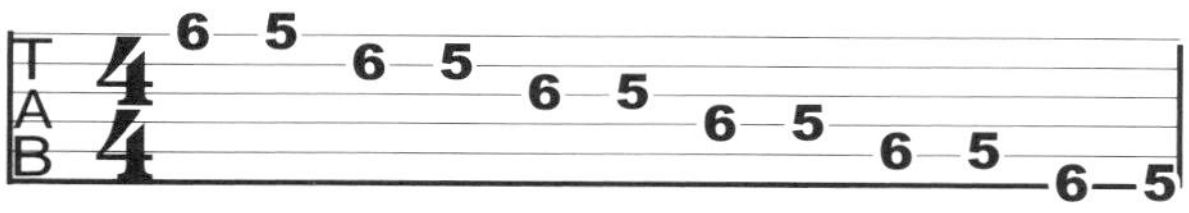

what you can do with your fingers

When you understand the basis of exercises 1 and 2 you can easily expand the idea into a full program of technical exercises that will give you great technique and excellent co-ordination. To make this easy, think of exercise 1 as the <u>1 - 2</u> exercise (1st finger, 2nd finger ex.) and exercise 2 as the <u>2 - 1</u> exercise. You have four basic right hand approaches as described on the previous page, so already this has grown into 8 exercises. The following chart shows all the possible variations; 2 finger variations; 3 finger variations; and, most important for overall technical fluency, 4 finger variations.

2 FINGERS

1 - 2	2 - 1
1 - 3	3 - 1
1 - 4	4 - 1
2 - 3	3 - 2
2 - 4	4 - 2
3 - 4	4 - 3

3 FINGERS

1 - 2 - 3	3 - 2 - 1
1 - 3 - 4	4 - 3 - 1
1 - 4 - 3	3 - 4 - 1
2 - 3 - 4	4 - 3 - 2
2 - 4 - 3	3 - 4 - 2
2 - 4 - 1	1 - 4 - 2

4 FINGERS - SET 1

1 - 2 - 3 - 4
1 - 2 - 4 - 3
1 - 3 - 2 - 4
1 - 3 - 4 - 2
1 - 4 - 2 - 3
1 - 4 - 3 - 2

4 FINGERS - SET 2

2 - 1 - 3 - 4
2 - 1 - 4 - 3
2 - 3 - 1 - 4
2 - 3 - 4 - 1
2 - 4 - 3 - 1
2 - 4 - 1 - 3

4 FINGERS - SET 3

3 - 1 - 2 - 4
3 - 1 - 4 - 2
3 - 2 - 4 - 1
3 - 2 - 1 - 4
3 - 4 - 2 - 1
3 - 4 - 1 - 2

4 FINGERS - SET 4

4 - 3 - 2 - 1
4 - 3 - 1 - 2
4 - 2 - 3 - 1
4 - 2 - 1 - 3
4 - 1 - 2 - 3
4 - 1 - 3 - 2

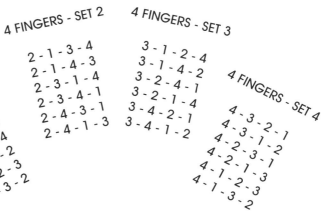

getting to know the notes

Before you start trying to make sense of your fingerboard, take a little time to understand the language of music. This language is based on the first seven letters of the alphabet A-B-C-D-E-F-G, with the possible addition of other characters - namely sharp (which is written ♯), and flat (which is written ♭). The diagram (fig.1) shows that the musical alphabet is a cycle of notes. When you reach the end of the alphabet you begin again at the beginning. In other words the note that follows G will be A.

The correct name for a note described simply as a letter of the alphabet, such as 'A', is 'A natural'. In practise this word natural is only really used by musicians when trying to distinguish an 'A natural', for example, from an 'A sharp'.

A vital concept to understand before any other, is that the distance (correct term - interval), between natural notes is not always the same. Some notes have a two fret distance - this interval is called a TONE, and some have a one fret distance - this interval is called a SEMITONE.

N.B. TONE = 2 frets
SEMITONE = 1 Fret.

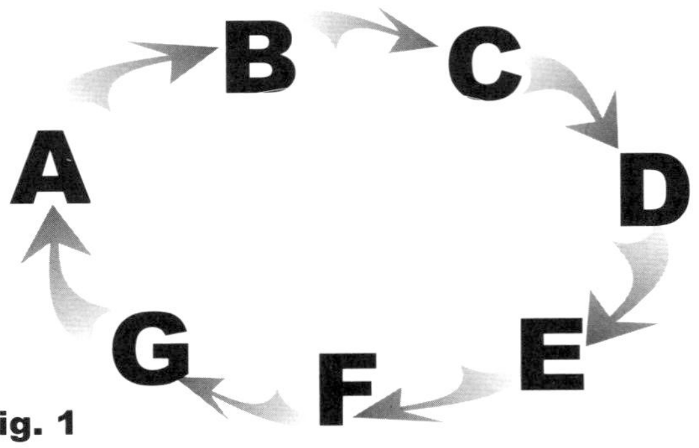

fig. 1

This may at first seem complicated but it is very easy because all you need to remember is:

ALL NATURAL NOTES are a TONE apart
EXCEPT FOR
B - C and E - F
which are a SEMITONE apart.

This fact will, of course, be true to all instruments and all music and so is vital for communication with other musicians.

early exploration *- one string at a time*

To begin with, let's look at the guitar string by string. Even though you will eventually be playing the guitar by keeping your hand in one or two places and playing from string to string going across the neck, it is easier to gain understanding of the notes by playing on one string.

Think of each string as a separate instrument, like having six pianos, all tuned from a different point.

Look at the diagram of the low E string. Note that at this point the only letters of the musical language are the natural note letters, no sharp or flat notes at this stage.

Practise playing (just use one or two fingers for now) each natural note in turn, call out the note name and climb the neck, note by note, until it is uncomfortable to go any further. Try again, only when you reach your

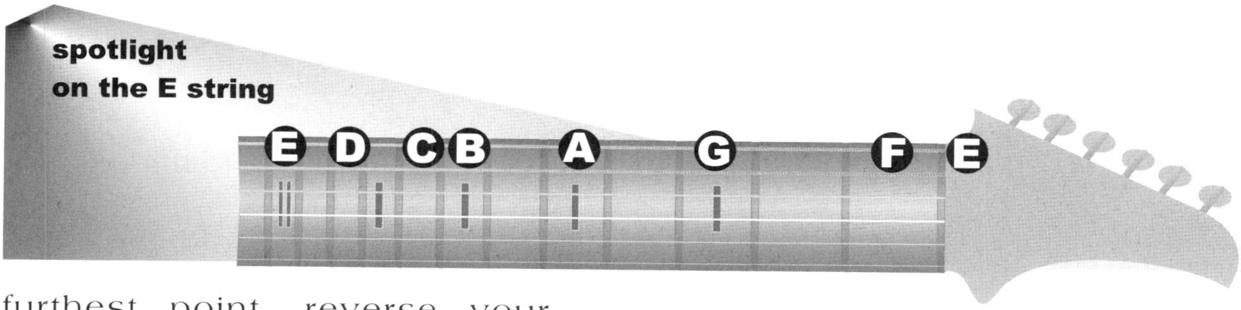

furthest point, reverse your direction, still calling out all the note names.

The initial purpose of this exercise is to learn the names of the notes. However, the letters you have been calling out are not a language in themselves - they are not music. Try the same exercise again, being careful to only play on the frets you previously played calling out the natural note names but this time listen to the language. That is, listen to the sound that each note makes and the sound of each note following on from the next. When you play every note name in sequence, you are actually playing a scale. It doesn't matter for now what that scale is called, just that scales are the building blocks of melody and melody is one of the main elements that create the language of music.

Explore each string - one at a time. Sometimes concentrate on what the notes are called and sometimes listen to the sounds you are creating. You're probably already having a listen to what happens when you break the sequence and jump from say, G to B or A down to F. Feel free to experiment although try and stick to only landing on Natural notes for now, otherwise you may get some unexpected sounds that put you off experimenting.

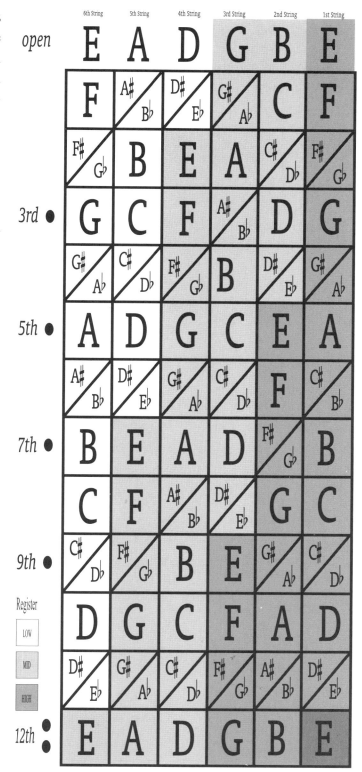

	6th String	5th String	4th String	3rd String	2nd String	1st String
open	E	A	D	G	B	E
	F	A♯ / B♭	D♯ / E♭	G♯ / A♭	C	F
	F♯ / G♭	B	E	A	C♯ / D♭	F♯ / G♭
3rd ●	G	C	F	A♯ / B♭	D	G
	G♯ / A♭	C♯ / D♭	F♯ / G♭	B	D♯ / E♭	G♯ / A♭
5th ●	A	D	G	C	E	A
	A♯ / B♭	D♯ / E♭	G♯ / A♭	C♯ / D♭	F	C♯ / B♭
7th ●	B	E	A	D	F♯ / G♭	B
	C	F	A♯ / B♭	D♯ / E♭	G	C
9th ●	C♯ / D♭	F♯ / G♭	B	E	G♯ / A♭	C♯ / D♭
	D	G	C	F	A	D
	D♯ / E♭	G♯ / A♭	C♯ / D♭	F♯ / G♭	A♯ / B♭	D♯ / E♭
12th ●●	E	A	D	G	B	E

Register: LOW, MID, HIGH

Living Together: The First Week

single line playing across the fingerboard

By learning the notes on the fingerboard you have become exposed already to simple single line playing and have heard one of the main elements of the musical language - scales. You should now be totally confident about defining both TONES and SEMITONES.

Well OK, just in case you've forgotten already, here it is again.

TONE = 2 FRETS
SEMITONE = 1 FRET.

Another important principle to establish is UP and DOWN. When musicians talk about UP and DOWN they are ALWAYS referring to SOUND. They are referring to the pitch of the notes. So UP is HIGHER in PITCH and DOWN is LOWER in PITCH. Play a note on your low E string such as F or G. Now play on your high E string - although your HAND has moved down (towards the floor) the notes you're playing are HIGHER in pitch and, therefore, you have gone UP musically. Looked at another way, if you play notes on the 1st, 2nd or 3rd frets of one string and move your hand along the neck towards your body, the pitch of the notes will be higher and you are therefore going UP in PITCH.

OK, you've easily read enough and done enough basic exercises to begin playing some music - let's never forget why you went out and bought a guitar!

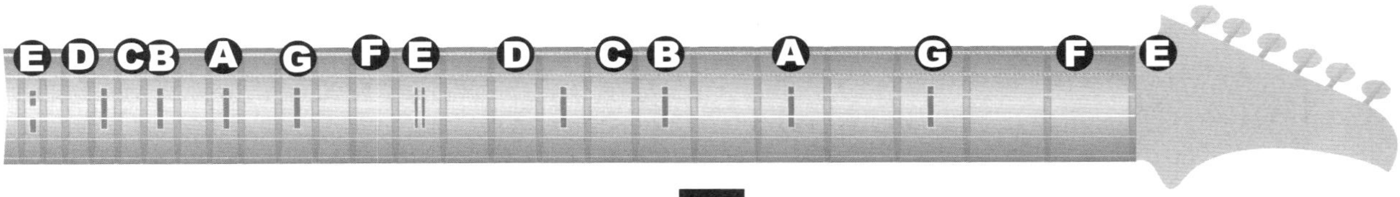

EXERCISE 1

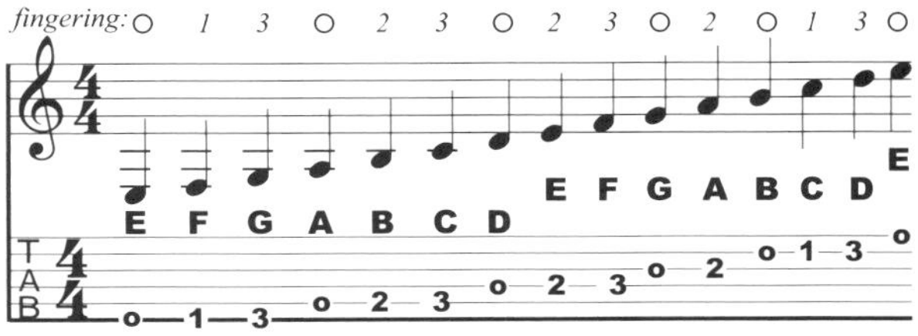

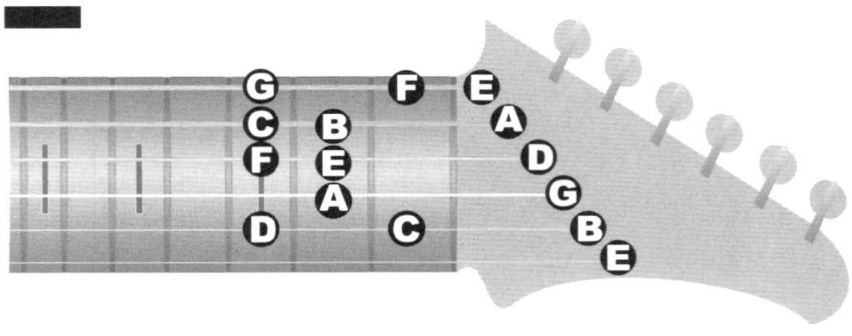

Play again the exercise you started with to learn the notes on your low E string. E-F-G-A-B-C-D. Have you noticed how 'Spanishy' this sounds, even if you're playing slowly. Well, all scales have their own character - to get the most from it however, you need to find a slightly more sensible way of playing it than on one string.

See exercise 1 at the bottom of page 13, which illustrates how you play these notes in a single position i.e. without moving your left hand. All of the open strings can be used making it even easier on the left hand fingers.

You are now playing a scale, called E Phrygian. Don't let this name bother you for now (although you can immediately use it to impress your friends). Not only are you playing E phrygian, you are also playing E phrygian across two octaves - impressive indeed.

As with your earlier form of this scale on one string, you should strive to find out what each note is called. Play up and down the scale calling out the note names.

As playing this scale without the need to move your left hand very much, is a hell of a lot easier than playing it up and down on one string you should now find it much easier to listen to the character and sound of the scale and therefore experiment with little tunes and ideas of your own - it's easy just play 3 or four notes in sequence and then back down, then try going up 6 and back down 3. To preserve the 'Spanish' flavour, make sure you start all your ideas on either the low open E, or the high open E.

spanish heat

Here are a couple of tunes, continuing the Spanish theme. Notice that they are created from the natural notes that you originally discovered on the E string. After you've played these two ideas, see if you can invent your own variations.

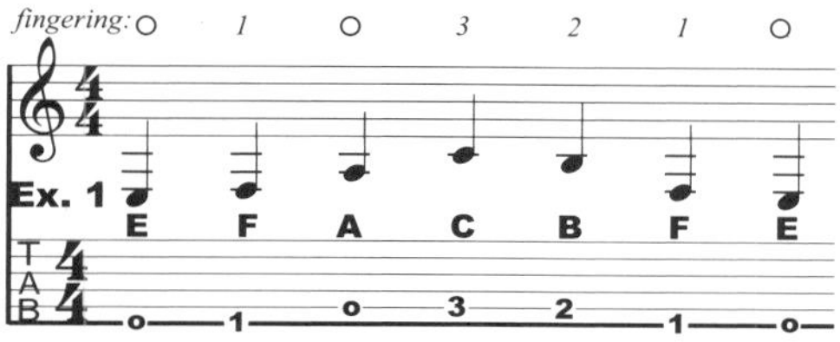

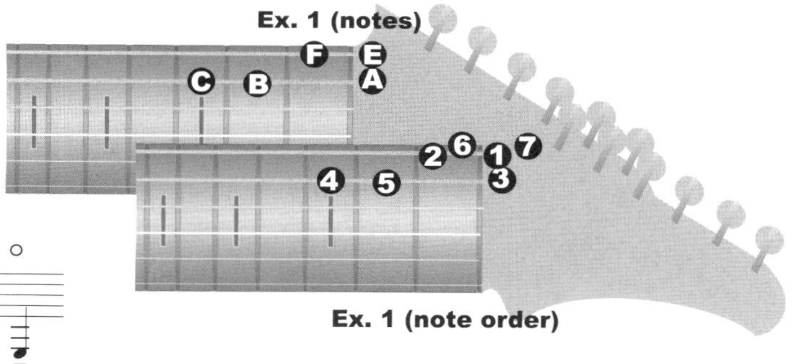

a natural minor

The scale illustrated below is called 'A' minor, or more correctly 'A' natural minor, as minor scales have a number of variations. The character of this scale is similar to Phrygian, although instead of sounding 'Spanishy', it is more moody and melancholy.

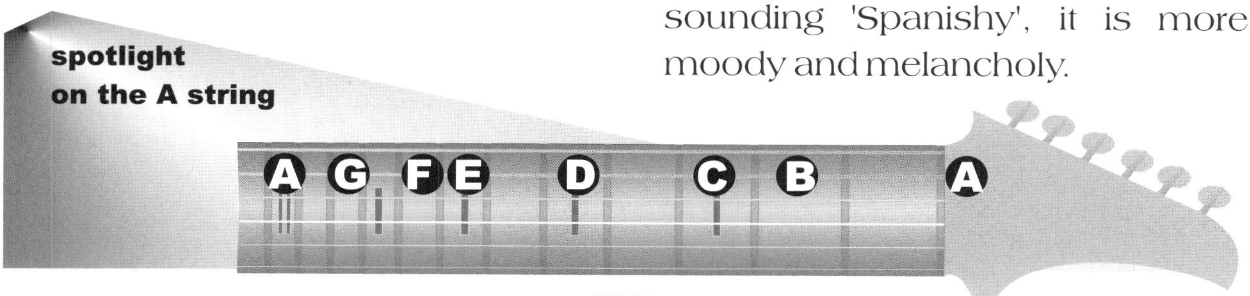

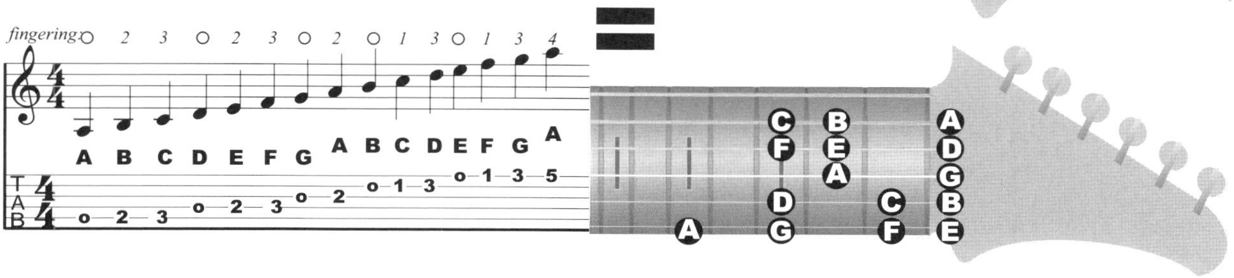

an easy introduction to chords

A chord is created by playing two or more notes - AT THE SAME TIME. You will already have played some sort of chords when you first picked up the guitar and strummed across all of the strings. If for some strange reason you've never tried this, do it now. Drag the pick swiftly across all six strings from the low E string to the high E string. You don't need to press any fingers down, all open strings will do. This is an example of a chord. It may not be that attractive a chord - as it's actually quite a complex chord - but it is a chord.

One of the reasons why so many people choose to learn guitar is that it is possible to play a large number of different chords by learning a few simple shapes. Having said this, I hope that by the end of this book I will have persuaded you to study chords musically rather than by being happy with getting away with a few shapes and patterns.

For now you will get a lot of pleasure from just one chord shape.

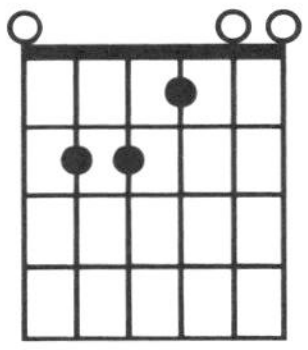

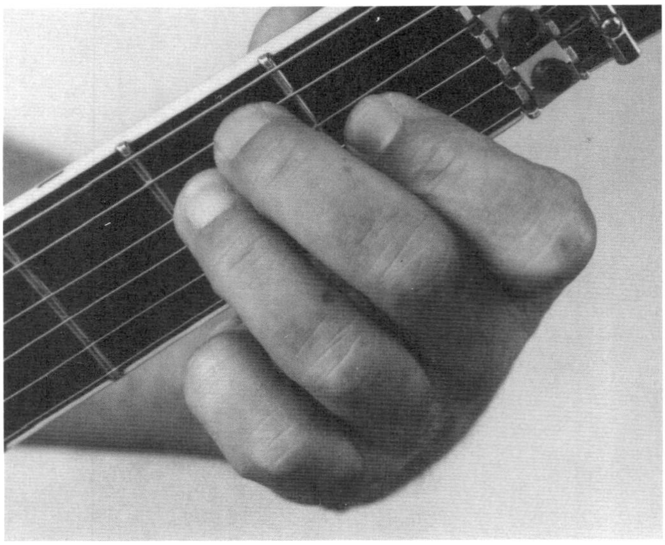

This chord is really important and useful but it's also really easy to play - no stretches, no funny shapes, just easy.

Remember, I said that this shape will be able to give you a lot of pleasure. Try this simple exercise for some instant music.

Play the shape in open position, as described above. Now move the three fingers used to press down the notes up (towards you) ONE fret. Resolve this idea back to the original position. Now, what was that? Sounds like our 'Spanish' idea is back in town! Now try again, first from the open position, next moving up one fret and then moving up two more frets. You have now created 3 different chords from just one simple shape. In addition to this you probably feel you could easily accompany a raunchy Spanish dancer - not a bad days work.

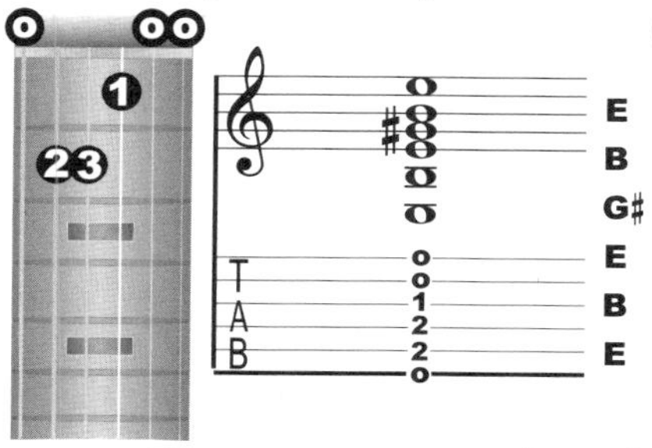

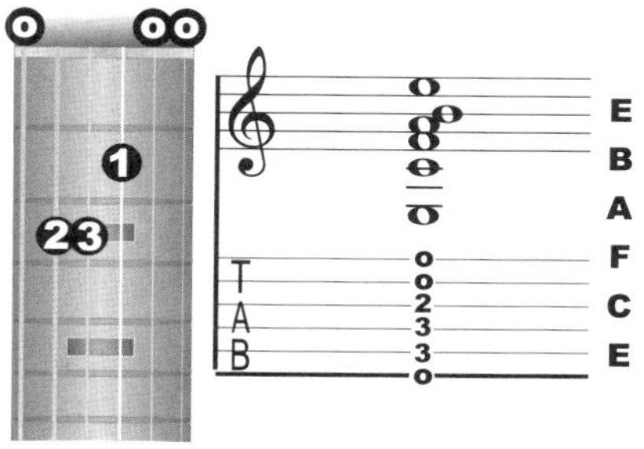

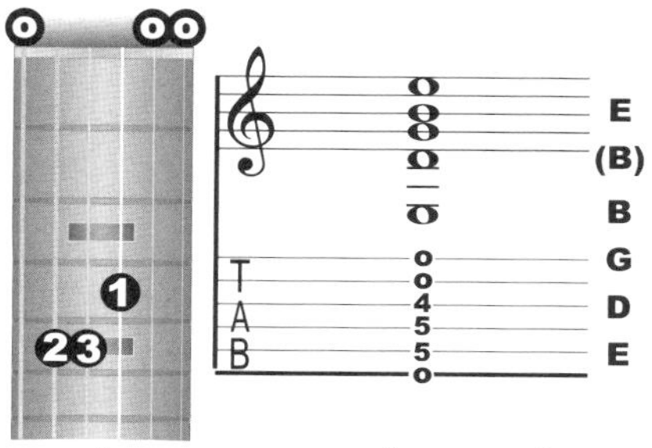

Try now and mix your E phrygian scale idea in with these three chords. Begin your journey by playing the E phrygian scale ascending (rising in pitch - from low E to mid E), followed by your first chord (open position E major). Pause on this chord, then play the same scale again followed by your second chord (up one fret), then play the scale again, followed by your third chord (up three frets), back to the 2nd chord, then back to E major to conclude. Try mixing these chords with the Spanish Heat ideas as well as your own variations. (This idea is notated below.)

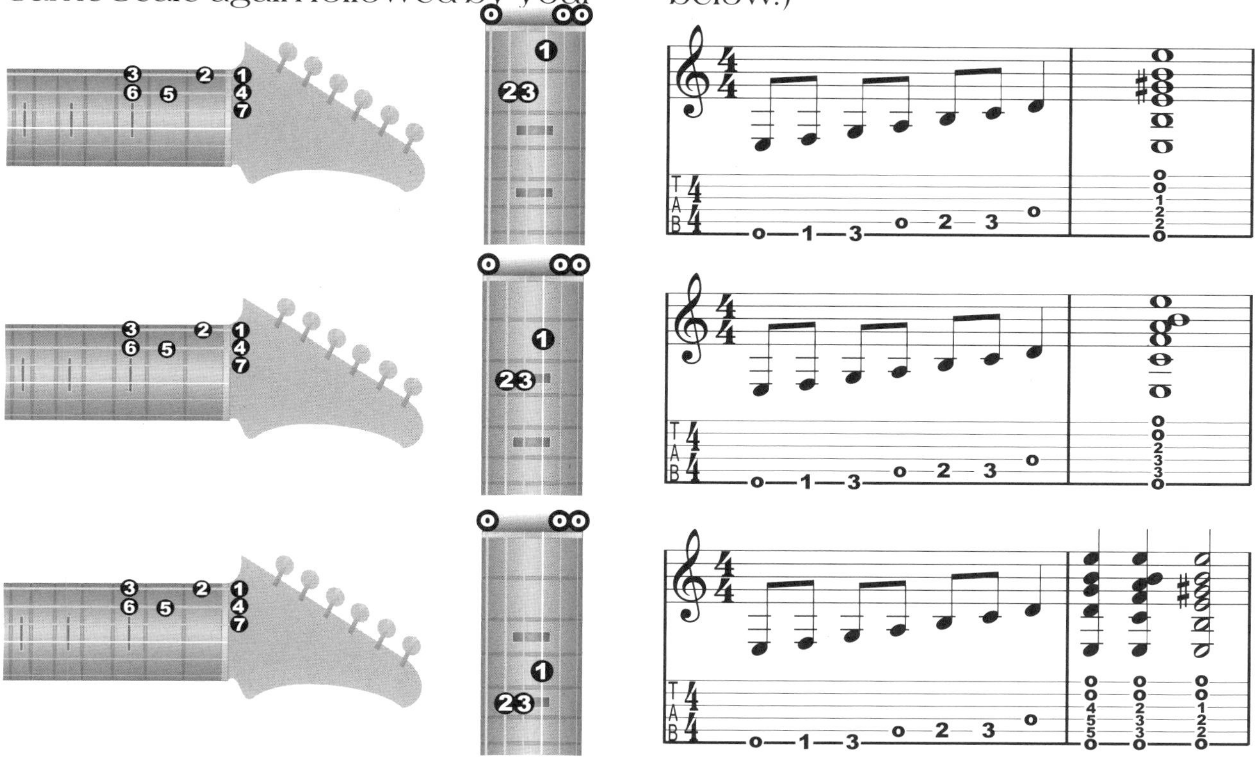

All these experiments should be explored and enjoyed. You are now hearing all the elements in the musical language; MELODY - scale ideas; HARMONY - chord shapes and hopefully, you've been adding a bit of your own RHYTHM, for spice! Easy to play - but very musical. (Do check the diagrams and notation carefully to make sure you are playing the correct shape in the correct place.)

more easy to play music

We can take this idea into another form and look at an idea that is just as easy for the left hand. In the following idea, the left hand only has to press 2 notes down and once again can keep the same shape moving up and down the finger board.

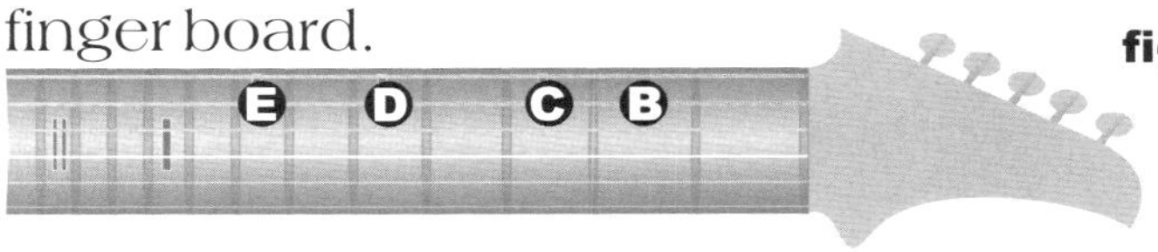

To get used to the 'progression' of the chords start by playing what is, in effect, the bass line to the progression (see fig. 1) E-D-C-B.

fig. 1

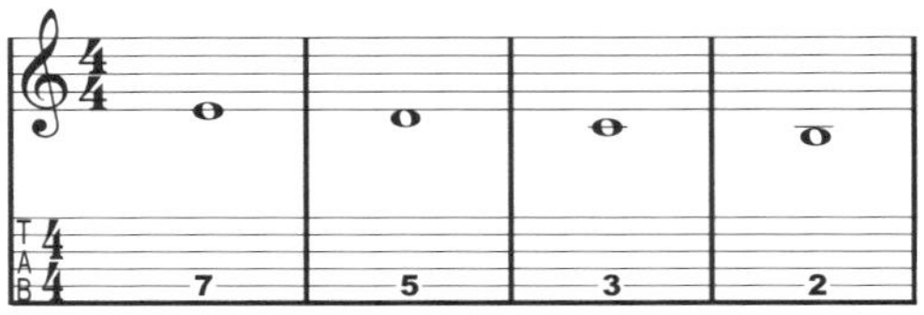

Now add the 2nd note played by the left hand - check the diagram for your exact position. Next, gently strum both the strings being played by the left hand (A string and D string) and also strum the G string and B string in the same movement. Practise the progression now with all four notes being heard - space the chords equally apart in time.

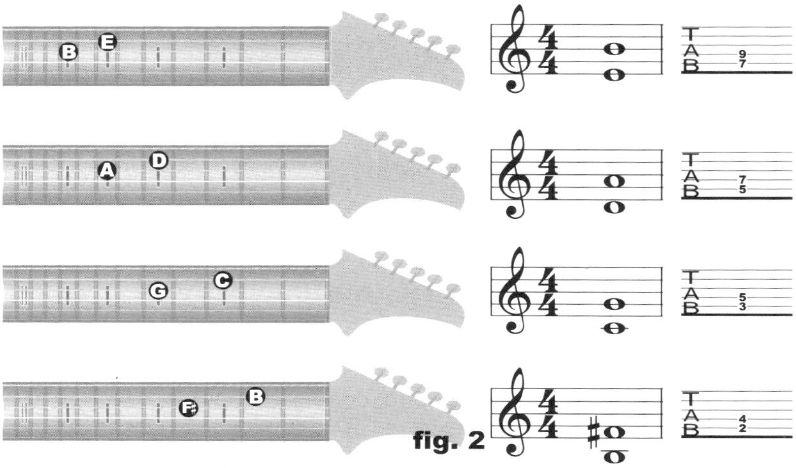

fig. 2

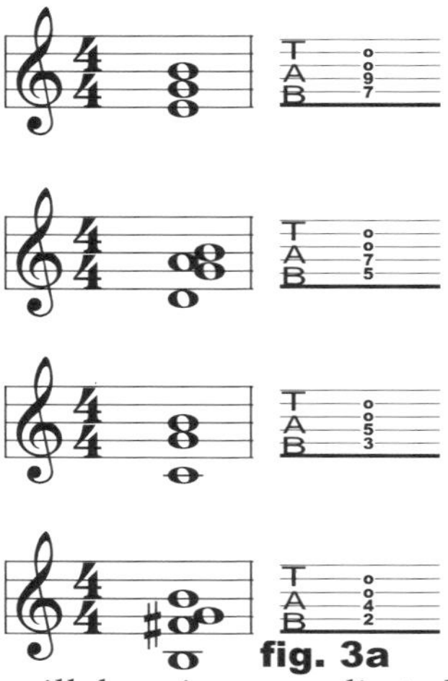

fig. 3a

Now, if you've worked on your pick technique a little, you should be able to pick the notes from each chord individually to create both a chord sound (created by allowing the notes to ring together) and a melody sound, created by the sequence of picking. You will be immediately familiar with this style of guitar playing. Again, easy but very musical. The picking sequence may take you a few days to get down but practise regularly and you'll soon have it.

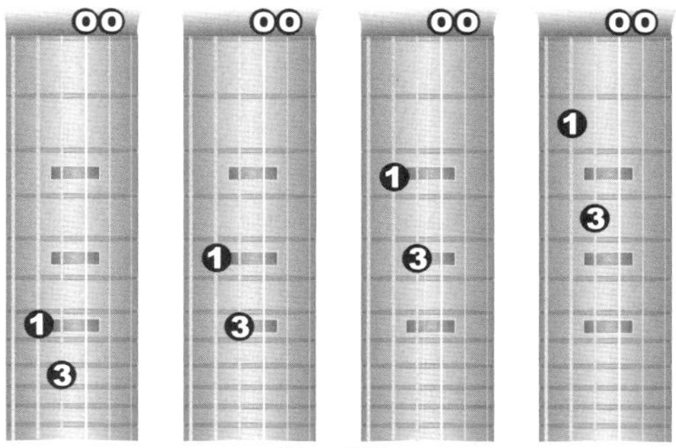

fig. 3b

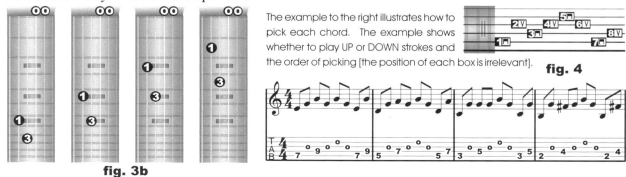

The example to the right illustrates how to pick each chord. The example shows whether to play UP or DOWN strokes and the order of picking [the position of each box is irrelevant].

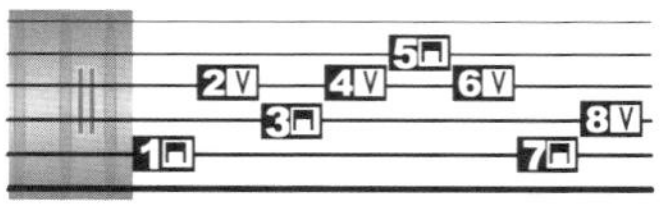

fig. 4

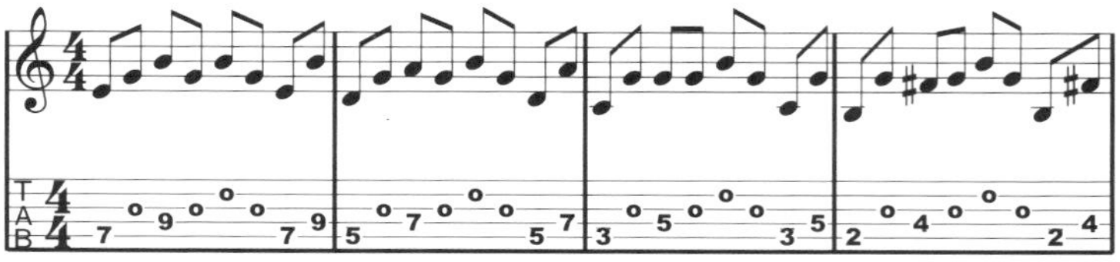

two hand co-ordination

We have seen so far how to bring both melody and harmony together. Any rhythm that you may have been adding along the way will probably have been a fairly 'hit and miss' affair.

As guitarists, we need to be expert in all elements of the musical language; MELODY, HARMONY and RHYTHM.

Although you will naturally play and feel certain rhythms and will already have been experimenting, the study of rhythm needs to begin away from the guitar. This is so that our understanding of how it works is not distracted by technical problems that will still persist in our right and left hands.

In addition to the basics of time-keeping and rhythm elements, as guitarists, we need to be very precise in our co-ordination between right and left hands. We can dramatically improve co-ordination by practising various rhythmic rudiments; tapping our hands on a table top etc.

I've borrowed the following from "Everything You Need To Know About Being A Drummer", - by Neil Martin (another book in the Beginners Series). These drum rudiments are tried and tested exercises that develop superb co-ordination between the right and left hands.

1.

2.

3.

4.

5.

6.

7.

8.

the arithmetic of rhythm

To start with, clap your hands when dealing with rhythm exercises. This is easy and natural - the only concept you need to be familiar with and develop is that, as the sound of a hand clap is short and percussive, we need a system where we can identify whether a note is imagined to sustain or whether there is a silence in the rhythm. When clapping hands, hold together if the note is intended as a sustain and hold hands apart if there is supposed to be silence. It is also a really good idea to sing rhythm, this is especially important if you've found clapping difficult to co-ordinate.

Try the following simple counting exercises, which will familiarise you with the basic elements of rhythm. You will quickly be aware that all the elements of rhythm are related to each other arithmetically. There's nothing too hard about this arithmetic, just 2 + 2 = 4 etc. Rhythm and time keeping are essential skills for all guitarists. It doesn't matter whether you're playing a punchy chord part or playing a solo - it all has to be played with accuracy and consistency. Use a metronome or drum machine frequently when you practise so that you're always thinking of the beat.

It is useful to introduce you to some music notation at this point. Rhythms are made up from arithmetically related elements. In other words; you have notes that last (sustain) for 4 beats, 2 beats, 1 beat, half a beat etc. Each of these elements has a name and a symbol. Learning the symbols is quite easy because there are only 5 or 6 that you need to remember.

Rhythm can become quite complex if the basic elements are mixed together. The most complex rhythms arise when a rhythm element is played off the beat (in the middle of two beats, or on any arithmetic division of the beat).

Playing off the beat is known as syncopation and will be dealt with a little later in this book.

For now, you need to become familiar with the basic elements:

1. The whole note

1 & 2 & 3 & 4 &

sustains for 4 beats

2. The half note

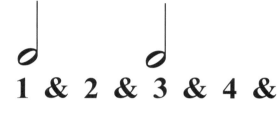

1 & 2 & 3 & 4 &

sustains for 2 beats

3. The quarter note

1 & 2 & 3 & 4 &

sustains for 1 beat. Put another way, the quarter note is taken to be the beat.

4. The eighth note

can be grouped in 2 or 4 with a crossbeam or written individually.

1 & 2 & 3 & 4 &

sustains for 1/2 beat.

When counting time, the shortest, or fastest element always needs to be counted, understood and felt. The body movement should also be motivated by this sub-division of the beat.

Settling Down
Looking to the Future

easy chords and strumming

On this page, you are going to learn some of the commonest chord shapes for guitar and some common chord progressions. These chords are all 'open' position chords which means that you incorporate open string notes in each chord. It usually means that your hand will be near the nut, with the fingers playing on the first, second and third frets.

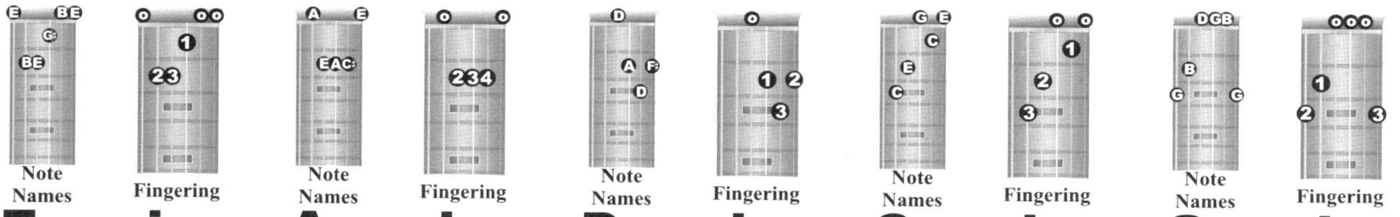

E major **A major** **D major** **C major** **G major**

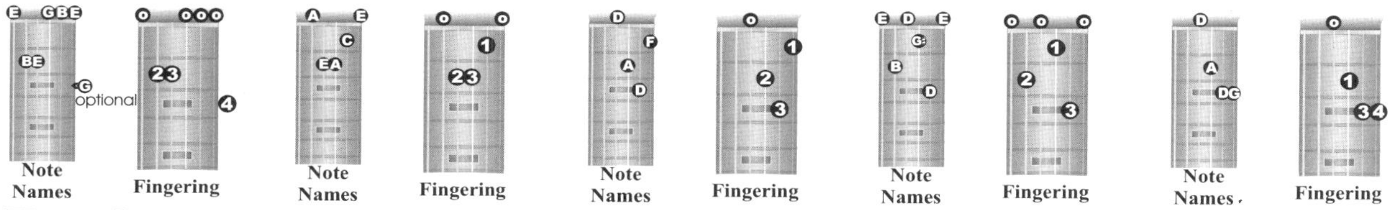

E minor **A minor** **D minor** **E7** **Dsus4**

First, you should practise each shape individually. Listen to the sound of the chord when you strum all of the strings, play each string separately to make sure all the notes are sounding and get the hand comfortable.

Second, you need to be able to change chord. The following chord progressions give you some practise at doing this, although for practise you should attempt all the possible chord changes that you can think of. You can even add the chords from pages 16 and 17.

When strumming the following progressions follow the advice on right hand technique discussed on page 6 but allow for a bigger movement. The exact rhythm doesn't matter for now although a drum machine keeping time would be of real benefit.

The following examples simply supply you with the chord symbols - this is how chords are normally written down in books and by other musicians that you will work with. There will be more on this later but for now remember that major chords are identified by a capital letter only, i.e. C major is simply C. Minor chords use a capital letter followed by a small m, i.e. D minor is simply Dm.

Strumming suggestion and rhythm

ex. 1: || G | C | D | D ||

ex. 2: || A | E | D | E ||

ex. 3: || Am | Dm | Am | Em ||

ex. 4: || A | D | E | E7 ||

ex. 5: || A | D | E | E7 ||

ex. 6: || Dsus | D | G | A ||

bar chords

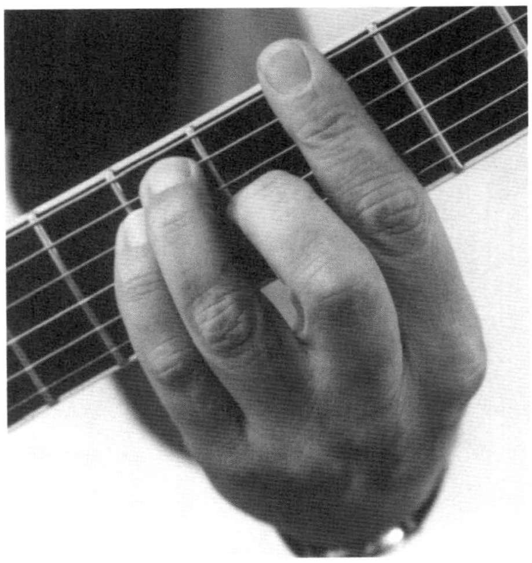

Bar chords are so named because one finger of the left hand (nearly always the first or index finger) is laid across the fingerboard - flat, straight and firm; like a bar. This 'bar' then acts like the nut in open position. You can then (provided you develop your stretch) play most of the shapes that you could play in open position (see page 20).

By far the most common and useful chord to use with the bar is the E major shape. It's also easy to know the chord name as the root is played by the bar on the low E string.

It may take a while before you find bar chords comfortable and before all the strings are pressed down effectively. Don't worry about this concentrate on the four shapes I've outlined in this section and practise changing from the 'E' shape to the 'A' shape. Do a little at first and build up so that eventually the whole process of forming the bar and maintaining its shape becomes easy.

Above shows the 'classic' bar chord shape and to the right shows the thumb 'round the neck approach.

the 12 bar blues

The 12 bar sequence or 12 bar blues is one of the commonest chord progressions in contemporary music.

It is very embarrassing not to know this progression as you will often be called on to jam (play without any preparation or rehearsal) with musicians you meet for the first time, using this progression.

It is useful also because it establishes the importance of the chords built on the 1st, 4th and 5th notes of the scale (more on this later). Chords built on these notes will sometimes be described as the I chord, the IV (4) chord and the V (5) chord. (Roman numberals are used if this is written down.)

Although these three chords are traditionally arranged in the order that we know as the 12 bar blues, they can be arranged in almost any order and structure to create an almost infinite number of compositions.

Run through the progression using open position chords and then try it using bar chords. Most important of all; learn the progression well and commit it to memory!

| A | A | A | A | D | D | A | A | E | D | A | E |

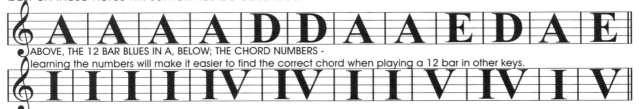

ABOVE, THE 12 BAR BLUES IN A, BELOW; THE CHORD NUMBERS - learning the numbers will make it easier to find the correct chord when playing a 12 bar in other keys.

| I | I | I | I | IV | IV | I | I | V | IV | I | V |

scales and keys

Earlier, when discussing the musical alphabet I mentioned that there are only seven letters of the alphabet required to describe music. However, by now you'll realise that the octave divides into 12 frets and therefore 12 notes. In nearly all types and styles of music the notes that make up the melody and harmony (chords) are derived from a set of seven notes only. The other five notes do not (usually) play a part.

These seven note sets are known as keys.

The result of playing all the notes of a key in sequence, from the most important note (the key note or key centre) until this same note is reached at its octave, is known as a scale.

The word key is usually used to describe and communicate which set of notes to play and a scale is all the notes of that 'set', played in sequence.

In music, there are different types of key (and scale) used by composers to create different moods and styles in music. The two most important types of key and scale are MAJOR and MINOR. In a simplistic way, the Major key is bright and positive and the Minor key is melancholy and sometimes plain miserable.

In addition to different types of key, composers may need to use different key centres, sometimes they may write a song in C major, which means the note C is revolved around and heard as the most important note. At other times a composer may use 'A' major, which means the note 'A', is the most important.

There are a number of reasons why they might do this. The easiest reason to understand is; imagine two singers, one has a high voice and the other not quite so high. The song is originally written for a high voice. The singer with the 'not so high' voice has to lower the key - lower the important note, in order to be able to sing the higher notes of the song.

Whatever the reason for a song being in a particular key, the bad news is that you need to be prepared for any key to be used - yep! you have to learn them all.

The examples on the next page show you how to play the major, minor, pentatonic and blues scales.

Memorise the finger patterns and then practise starting the scales from a different note each time you practise them.

LEARN YOUR KEY SETS; KNOWN AS KEY SIGNATURES

C MAJOR - All Natural Notes C-D-E-F-G-A-B

G	MAJOR	1 sharp note	G	A	B	C	D	E	F♯
D	MAJOR	2 sharps	D	E	F♯	G	A	B	C♯
A	MAJOR	3 sharps	A	B	C♯	D	E	F♯	G♯
E	MAJOR	4 sharps	E	F♯	G♯	A	B	C♯	D♯
B	MAJOR	5 sharps	B	C♯	D♯	E	F♯	G♯	A♯
F♯	MAJOR	6 sharps	F♯	G♯	A♯	B	C♯	D♯	E♯
F	MAJOR	1 flat note	F	G	A	B♭	C	D	E
B♭	MAJOR	2 flats	B♭	C	D	E♭	F	G	A
E♭	MAJOR	3 flats	E♭	F	G	A♭	B♭	C	D
A♭	MAJOR	4 flats	A♭	B♭	C	D♭	E♭	F	G
D♭	MAJOR	5 flats	D♭	E♭	F	G♭	A♭	B♭	C
G♭	MAJOR	6 flats	G♭	A♭	B♭	C♭	D♭	E♭	F

major scale

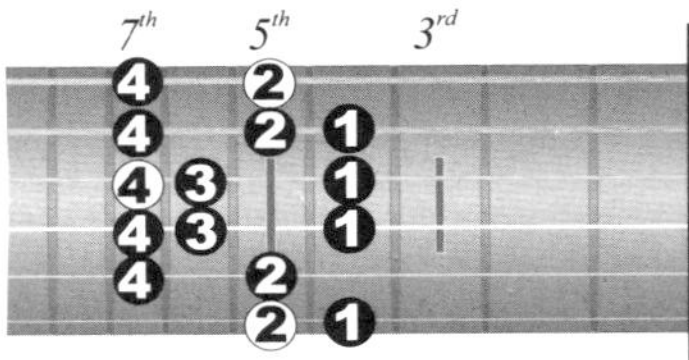

The major scale is really the mother of all scales. Learn this very carefully. When you know the finger pattern, try moving around the fingerboard - playing the same scale in different keys.

N.B. The graphic illustrations on this page show the position of each finger and the finger number. The reversed numbers show the KEY note.

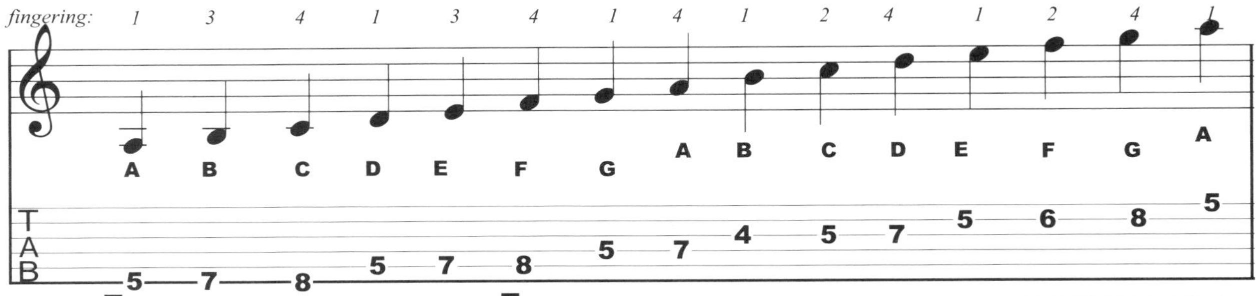

minor scale

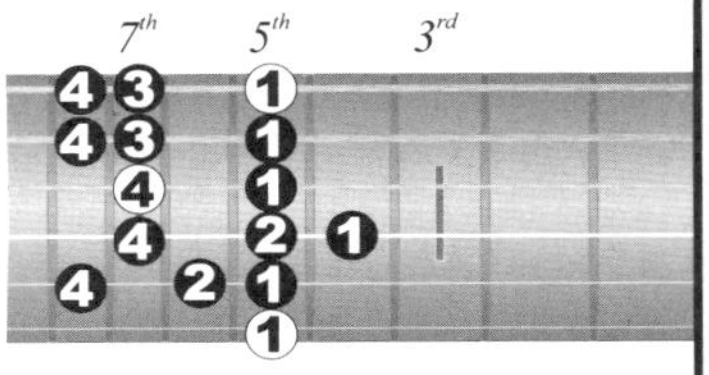

The minor scale, or in this case, the 'natural minor' scale is derived from the major scale. If you take any major scale and play a scale from its 6th note - the result will be the natural minor scale. You can also have a harmonic minor scale, which is identical except that the 7th note is sharp (or major), and the melodic minor which has a sharp 6th and 7th when ascending and is the same as natural minor descending.

N.B. Play all the scales on this page starting from the lowest note to the highest (ascending) and starting from the highest note to the lowest (descending).

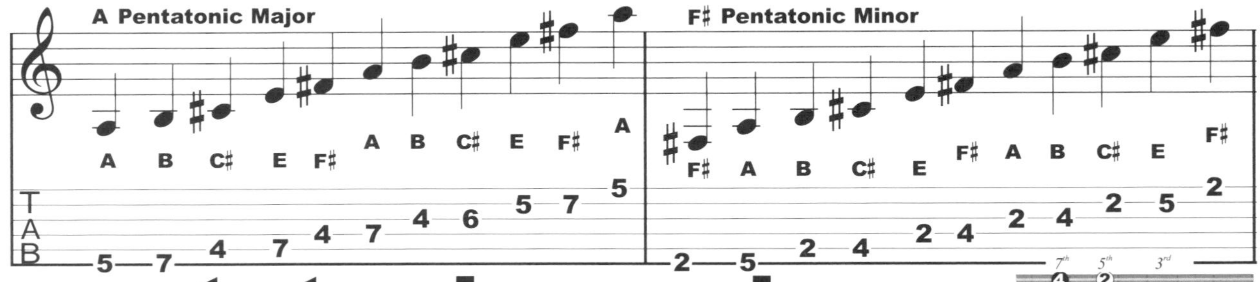

pentatonic scales

A pentatonic scale is a five note scale. It is derived from the major scale. If you take a major scale and 'miss out' the 4th and 7th notes you get a the major pentatonic. The pentatonic, like all other scales is a family of scales. This family comes about because you can create a 'new' scale by beginning on a different note of the scale. The major and minor pentatonic scales are the most important and so it is worth remebering that to create a minor pentatonic you can take a natural minor scale and 'miss out' the 2nd and 6th notes.

N.B. There are two approaches you can take when working out the different scale variations. 1. You can use the same notes (stay in the same key) and start from different notes of the scale - changing the key centre (as in the notation and tab example above). 2. You can keep the starting note or key centre the same. The five examples to the right illustrate the 'family' of pentatonic scales all starting on the note A.

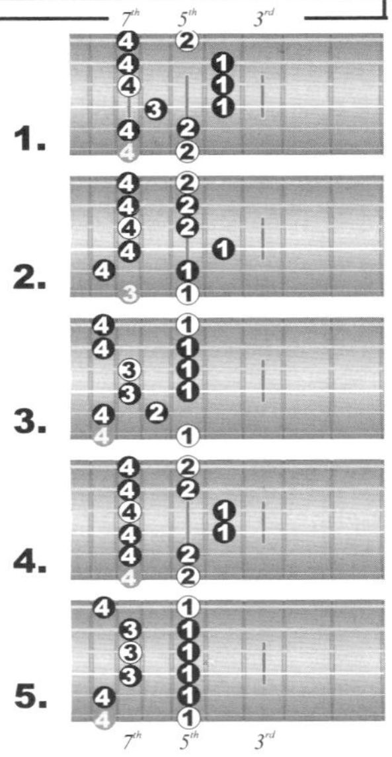

putting scales into practise

the major scale

The major scale tends to produce riffs that are bright and chirpy. Don't worry if you can't play the examples very quickly or even with accurate timing just listen to the notes to understand each scales character.

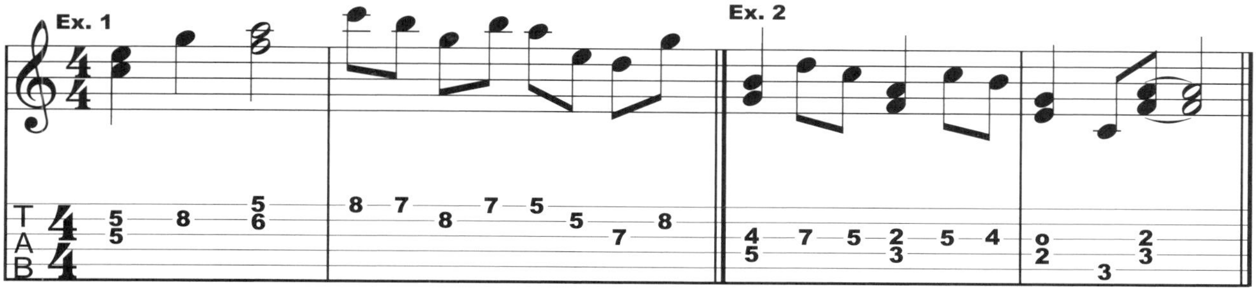

the minor scale

The minor scale is good for creating moody riffs. Both the examples below make use of both the 3rd and 6th notes of the scale. These two notes contribute most to this moody effect.

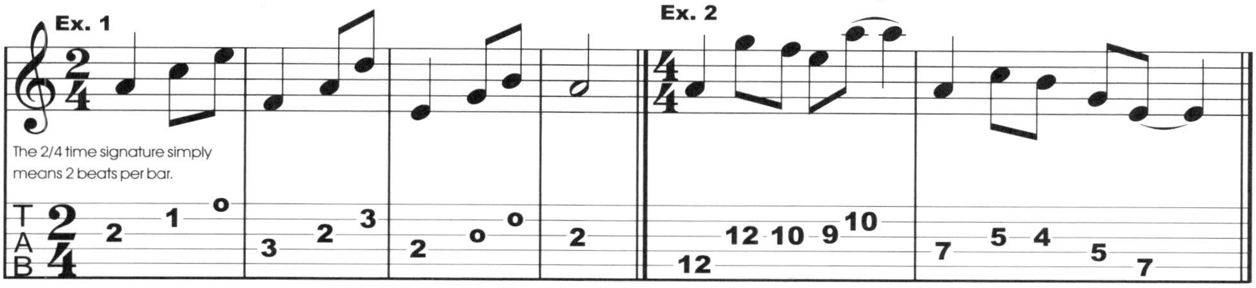

the pentatonic and blues scales

Ex. 1 and 2 are pure minor pentatonic ideas that can be played at various speeds and developed into good rock licks - remember the purpose of these examples is to introduce you to the *character* of scales.

Ex. 3 is a blues idea. The blues scale is the same as a minor pentatonic (see fig. 5 on page 23 and the F♯ minor pentatonic example) with the addition of a sharp 4th between the 4th and 5th notes of the scale (marked with * on Ex. 3). The idea features a blues 3rd bend where you start on the written note (G) and, slowly and teasingly bend towards G♯. The timing of the bend is a matter of personal taste but generally start slowly.

building chords

You already know that chords are created when you play two or more notes at the same time.

Most chords are built from a scale by taking every other note of the scale. For example, if you take the scale of C major; C - D - E - F - G - A - B - (C) and, beginning with the note C add E and add G you get a chord of C major. Another way of looking at this is to number each note of the scale 1 - 7 (the octave would start again at 1). By looking at the number of every other note of the scale you can see that a chord contains the 1st note, which is then called THE ROOT NOTE, the 3rd note - THE THIRD and the 5th note - THE FIFTH.

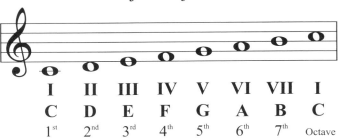

These three note chords are called TRIADS.

The Scale of C major

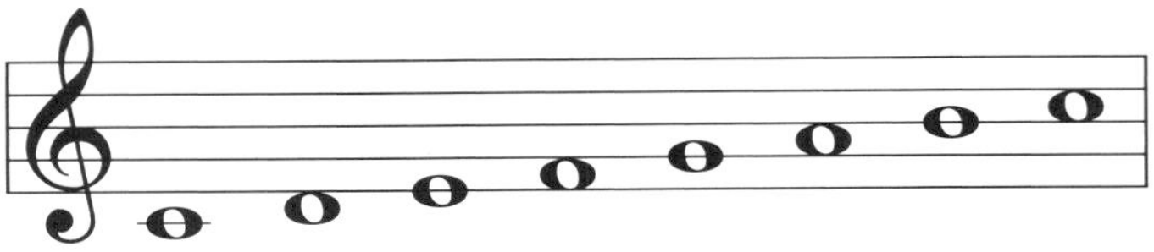

The Arpeggio of C major (The chord notes in sequence) ***The Chord of C major***

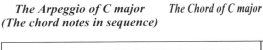

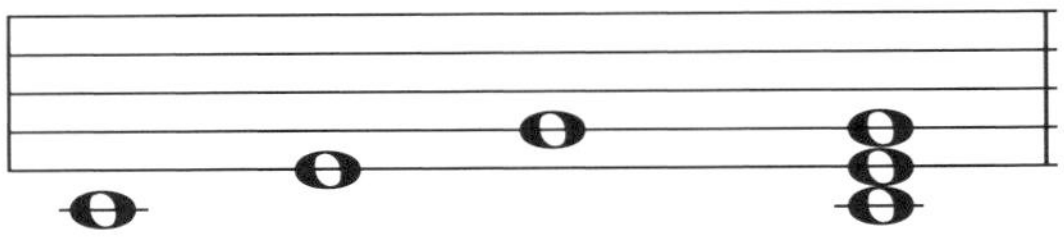

how to work out the chords for any key

As you know from the section 'Scales and Keys', most pieces of music are in one key for the length of the song or section of song. The chords used in the song must therefore only use notes that exist in that particular key. So, if you know what key a song is in you can then easily work out what chords the song can use.

To work out the harmony of a key (the available chords) consider that each note of the scale can become the root of a new chord and then find the third note and fifth note above each root using only the notes found in the key you're playing in. You therefore have 7 triads available in any key. Fig. 1 shows in detail how the first two chords are formed, fig. 2 give the full list for G major.

The scale of G major

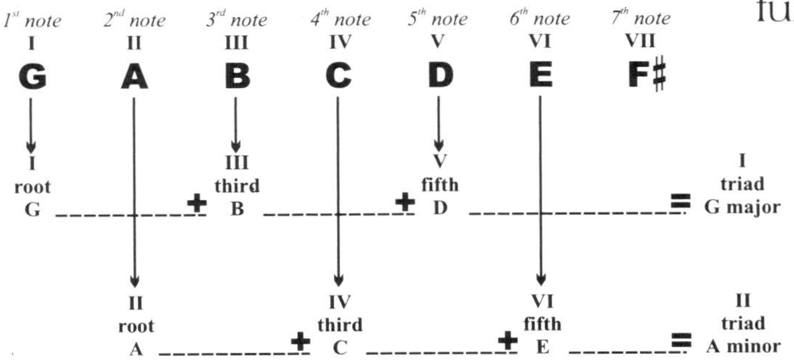

fig. 1

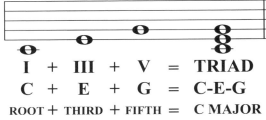

degree	ROOT	THIRD	FIFTH	CHORD NAME
I	G	B	D	G major
II	A	C	E	A minor
III	B	D	F♯	B minor
IV	C	E	G	C major
V	D	F♯	A	D major
VI	E	G	B	E minor
VII	F♯	A	C	F♯ diminished

fig. 2

all the triads

The following example shows how to construct all the different types of triad. Strictly, there are four types of triad - MAJOR - MINOR - DIMINISHED - AUGMENTED, we will add a fifth 3 note chord, namely the suspended 4th chord or sus 4 (usually just called 'sus'). In this chord the 4th replaces the 3rd of the chord.

MAJOR, MINOR, diminished, augmented. (sus 4 chord)

To understand the construction of triads you need to look at the number of semitones (1 fret intervals) from the Root to the Third and to the Fifth.

MAJOR: Root to 3rd = 4 semitones, to 5th = 7 semitones
MINOR: Root to 3rd = 3 semitones, to 5th = 7 semitones - so, to make a major chord into a minor chord, find the third and flatten (lower) it by one semitone.
DIMINISHED: Root to 3rd = 3 semitones, to 5th = 6 semitones
AUGMENTED: Root to 3rd = 4 semitones, to 5th = 8 semitones

THE SUSPENDED 4TH CHORD:
Root to 4th = 5 semitones, to 5th = 7 semitones.

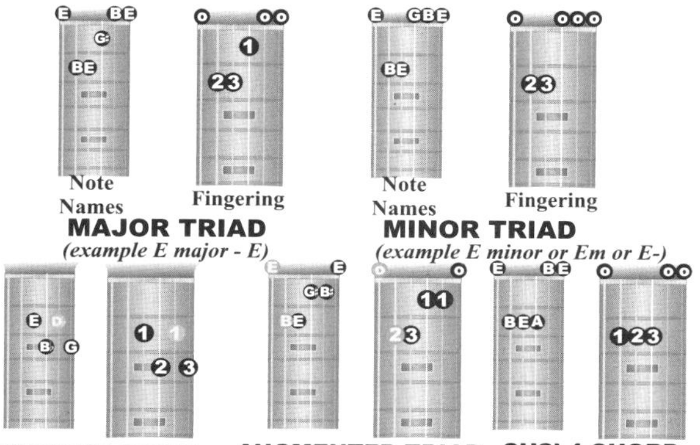

MAJOR TRIAD *(example E major - E)*

MINOR TRIAD *(example E minor or Em or E-)*

DIMINISHED TRIAD *(example E dim or E°) (E°7 if you include the greyed out notes)*

AUGMENTED TRIAD *(example E augmented or Eaug or E+ or E+5)*

SUS' 4 CHORD *(example E suspended 4th or Esus4 or Esus)*

expanding the chord sound

OK, so you understand how a triad is created but what about all those rich, incredible sounds you hear on records?

The vast majority of bigger chords simply start with a triad and 'build' or add notes on top. Thinking of numbers, or scale degrees, take the triad; ROOT, THIRD and FIFTH and add the SEVENTH note of the scale. You can take this further by adding the NINTH either in addition to the SEVENTH or instead of. You can continue by adding the 11th and even the 13th note of the (two octave) scale. The name of the chord will be taken from the last note added, e.g. G7 or C9 etc.

For the purposes of this book I will only show you in detail how to construct the THREE TYPES OF SEVEN CHORD.

MAJOR 7 CHORD
ROOT - MAJOR 3RD - PERFECT FIFTH - MAJOR 7TH

MINOR 7 CHORD
ROOT - MINOR 3RD - PERFECT FIFTH - MINOR 7TH

DOMINANT 7 CHORD
ROOT - MAJOR 3RD - PERFECT FIFTH - MINOR 7TH

N.B. Major 3rd = 4 semitones   Minor 3rd = 3 semitones
Perfect 5th = 7 semitones   Major 7th = 11 semitones   Minor 7th = 10 semitones

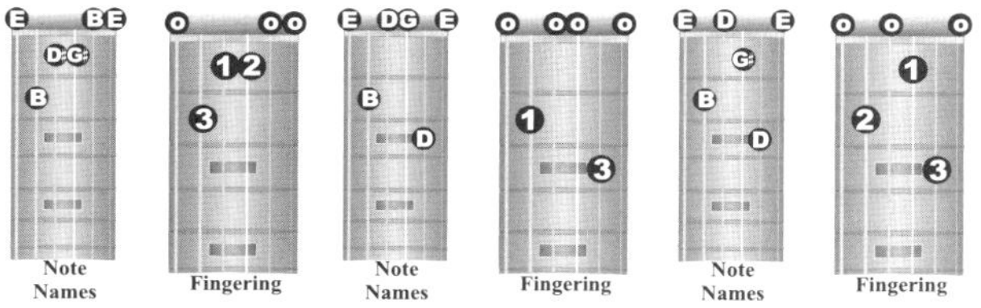

E maj 7 (E major 7)   **Em7 (E minor 7)**   **E7 (E dominant 7)**

N.B. [Em7 & E7] - The 'D' played with the 3rd finger on the 'B string' can be left out allowing the open 'B' to sound. Both are correct.

looking ahead - *inversions and voicing*

One idea I'd like to encourage is, that as you progress, you take more and more interest in understanding chord construction. Try not to rely 100% on shapes and patterns. Using the same shapes for the same chords all of the time will eventually leave your sound stale.

Basically, if you understand how to put chords together and if you have really learned your fingerboard and where to find notes, you can invent new ways of playing chords every time you pick up the guitar.

One point to remember is that the notes in chords can be placed in any order and can be spaced any way that you like. If the lowest note you play changes from the root to the third, this is called 1st inversion and if the lowest note you play is the 5th then it is called the 2nd inversion. Inverting chords adds to the variety of chord sounds.

rhythm, time keeping and counting

On page 19, I introduced you to the basics of rhythm and counting. Over the next couple of pages you will be encouraged to really study this subject.

All musicians and band members need to be good at rhythm and time-keeping, even though it's the drummer and bass player who will carry the responsibility in this area. If you are to be a confident player, whether laying down a rhythm part or screaming through a solo, you need to be good at keeping time.

Try and use a drum machine or metronome when playing - these tools really work and are worth a small investment. Also learn to count and tap your foot on the beat. You may find this is difficult to do at first, after all you've got two hands to concentrate on and now I'm asking you to tap your foot and count as well. However, slow down - be patient and build your skills slowly and progressively.

The addition of the tie, the dot and rests (silence) that are outlined in these pages will dramatically increase what is possible rhythmically for you and, if you work hard at your counting while learning the exercises, your time-keeping ability will rapidly develop.

Sing, clap and play (both on single notes and as chords) all the exercises.

the tie

This is a curved line that connects two successive notes of the same pitch and unites them into a single sound equal to their combined duration's. It has three uses.

1. To connect two notes separated by a bar line. (fig. 1)
2. To produce values that cannot be indicated by a single note on its own. (fig. 2)
3. To illustrate beat groupings (making music easier to read. (fig. 3)

fig. 1 **fig. 2** **fig. 3**

In this first figure, the tie is used to enable a note to sustain 'through' a bar line; i.e. the sound sustains from beat 3 of the first bar, through to beat 3 of the second bar.

Figure 2 shows how a tie can create a length of sound that cannot be expressed as a single symbol. In this case the sound is equal in length to 5

In figure 3. the tie is used to allow the eye to easily locate each beat (grouped here in pairs of eighth notes). This makes reading at sight much easier.

the dotted note

When a dot is placed after a note head, the length of that note is increased - BY HALF. e.g. a dotted half note is equal in length to a half note and a quarter note. The following examples should make the function of the dot clear. Follow the counting carefully to make sure you understand.

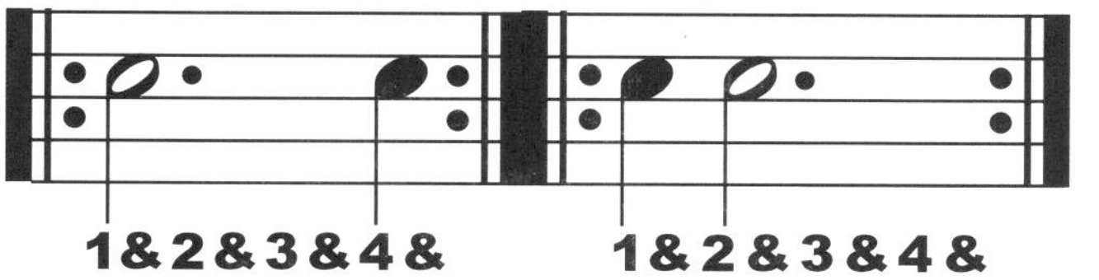

In the example below, notice that whereas the normal quarter note lasts for 2 eighth note counts, the dotted quarter note lasts for 3 eighth note counts (one +

Careful with the above; dotted notes and tied notes!

the sound of silence

Silence is a really useful tool in music. This is because it creates contrast with sound. Imagine the drummer just playing 4 to the bar on his kick drum, you wait till the 4& before letting rip with your screeching power chord - hold the chord for a beat and chop it dead - dramatic or what?

The only problem with silence, or rests - as periods of silence are called in music, is that we need to be good at counting. When you stop playing (rest) it's easy to lose your place - you must keep counting. Work really hard on the exercises below - use single notes or chords anywhere on the guitar and make sure that there is silence when a rest is marked.

The following examples illustrates the importance of silence (notated by rest symbols) in music. You will also discover that allowing for silence in music, puts your counting ability to the test in a big way! Don't forget that you will need to stop the previous note from ringing (damp the string) by touching with the right hand or taking the pressure off the left hand finger.

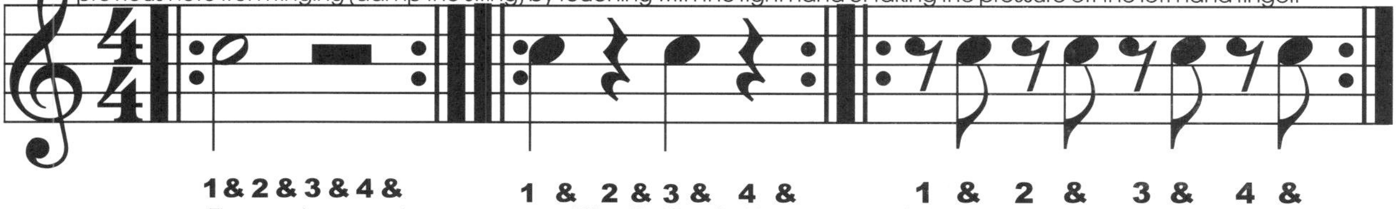

The next examples are more difficult. The first is a very useful rhythm. By damping your notes on the 2nd and 4th beats - the snare drum will sound huge. For this illusion to work, your first note must run right up to the 2nd beat, i.e there must be no gap between your note and the snare beat.

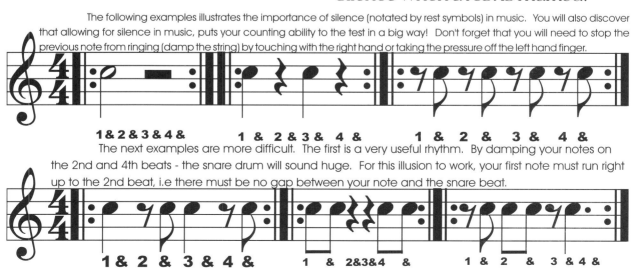

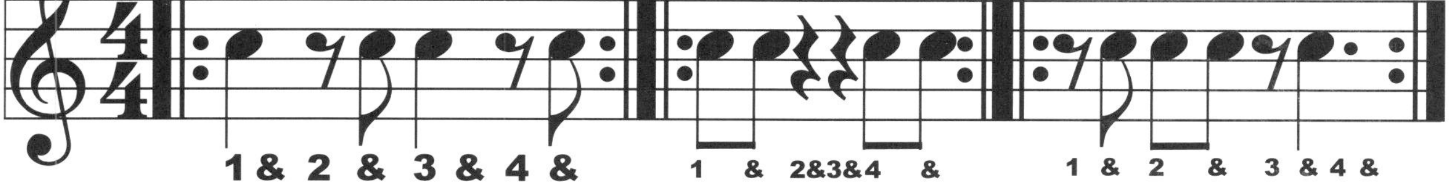

hearing and jamming

Despite investing all your money in your guitar and amp and all your time into getting your fingers to work properly, your most precious possessions are your ears. As with anything connected with the study of music, your ears need training.

Your objective is to be able to listen to musical sound and recognise what you hear exactly. This means, in practise, that if you hear a riff or melody you could, on listening, play that riff or melody on the guitar. You also need to be able to recognise chords. This is at first more difficult but you can quickly recognise different types of chord by their special characteristics and you'll also soon recognise common chord progressions.

Understanding Melody

The way to train your ear is to start with the major scale. Everything you hear will relate to this scale - for the time being at least. It is not expected that you can somehow 'know' what a note is called by listening to a sound without a reference point. (There are some people who *can* do this and they are said to have perfect pitch.) So we need a reference point or starting note. This will be the case if you're working out a record or working with a band - so always find a starting note or the key note and relate everything to this (known as relative pitch).

Each note of a melody will be a specific interval or distance in pitch from the preceding note. By learning the sound of all intervals and by associating a fingering for all intervals on the guitar you can gradually gain great confidence in playing what you hear.

Use your voice to sing the interval sounds. Only by singing sound (it doesn't matter whether or not you have a good voice) can you be certain that you are really understanding what you hear.

The INTERVALS of the Major Scale

- C — *OCTAVE* — **C**
- C — *Major 7th* — **B** — *Minor 7th* — **B♭**
- C — *Major 6th* — **A** — *Minor 6th* — **A♭**
- C — *Perfect 5th* — **G** — *Diminished 5th* — **G♭**
- C — *Perfect 4th* — **F**
- C — *Major 3rd* — **E** — *Minor 3rd* — **E♭**
- C — *Major 2nd* — **D** — *Minor 2nd* — **D♭**
- C

The remaining INTERVALS (learn only when Major and Perfect intervals are understood).

First, listen to the key note (in the example 'C'). Then listen to each note in turn - always with reference to the key note. Then, sing the key note followed by each note in turn. As you sing, think of the interval name, so that you associate the sound with the name e.g. (i) Play C, then play E - listen carefully, (ii) sing C, then sing E - think of the interval name, 'major 3rd' and (iii) check that you sang correctly.

Second, you must understand and recognise harmonic intervals, that is, two notes played together. As you will have to play these 2 note 'chords' on the guitar, you will also become aware of the way you finger each interval.

really hearing chords - *different chord types*

You have probably already got used to the difference in sound between a major and minor chord. To find out if you really can tell the difference, record a few examples of major and minor chords on a cassette player and write down what you play. Put the tape and paper away for a few days and then listen to the tape. Do you always know whether you're hearing a major or minor chord? Don't worry if you get caught out a little to start with - like anything else this is something you have to practise.

You can do the same for other types of chord. The main chord types to recognise are: **MAJOR, MINOR, DOMINANT 7, MAJOR 7, MINOR 7. DIMINISHED AND AUGMENTED** (see page 26). The 'sus 4' chord is also easy to hear and an important chord.

some common progressions

With only seven principal chords in any key it is inevitable that combinations of chords, or chord progressions, are going to be used time and time again. It is quite easy to learn by sound the common chord progressions. Play frequently the examples given and learn them by number (this is so that you immediately recognise the progression if you come across them in another key).

1. |I |IV |V |V7| **e.g. |A |D |E |E7|** *In A major*

2. |II|V |V7|I | **e.g. |Am|D|D7|G|** *In G major*

3. |I |VI |II |V | **e.g. |C|Am|Dm|G|** *In C major*

4. |I |VI |IV|V7| **e.g. |C|Am|F|G7|** *In C major*

5. |I |VII|VI|V7| **e.g. |Am|G|F|E7|** *In A minor*

6. |I |IV |VII|III|VI |II |V |V7 |
e.g. |Am|Dm|G|C|F|B dim|Esus|E7|
In A minor

putting chords to a melody

It's quite common in a band, or pre-band situation, to find yourself having to invent a chord progression to a melody line. Vocalists often have a few melodies but no idea what chords should accompany them.

This can seem quite a daunting task at first, except that you now have quite a lot of chord knowledge (if not - revise pages 25 and 26).

Melodies will contain 'principal' notes. These are notes that are either stressed (i.e. on a strong beat) or are held for longer than other notes. Either way, these principal notes will be heard 'with' the chord. Find out what notes these are, by getting the vocalist to 'hold' the note and find it on the guitar. Nine times out of ten, these principal notes will want to be treated as either the fifth or third of the chord. So, if the vocalist's note is 'A', you would treat this 'A' as either the fifth of a D major or D minor chord, or as the third of an 'F major' chord. It's not usually a good idea to treat the vocalist's note as a root note, as this will sound monotone - however the 'punks' used this to good effect, so don't ignore the possibility.

There are other possibilities and as you learn more about chords you will become aware of these naturally.

The Seven Week Itch
Getting Into A Band!

fitting in

It can be pretty nerve-racking trying to get into your first band. Understanding a little about the band and especially not fearing other musicians will help. Always remember you will be one member of a team, even when you solo it's not you against the world but you reflecting the song and the type of band you've just joined.

Other people will expect you to be good at getting a sound - this means understanding your equipment as well as having ideas. The sound(s) you develop will be your trademark - just make sure you can reproduce these sounds when it matters.

Make sure you take your ears with you to an audition or rehearsal or gig. What I mean is, listen to what others are doing and saying and play guitar parts that suit the song and the band.

the vocalist

Meet your first big problem in life. Tread very carefully when dealing with this species because they'll cry and stamp their feet if they don't get their way. The vocalist is never wrong, at least never tell them they're wrong. Suggest an alternative for them to try when they're in the mood.

The best thing to hope for with a vocalist is that they sound different. When trying to get a band noticed it really helps to have a distinctive vocal sound. If they can actually sing as well, then you've found your man (or woman, of course).

In addition, the vocalist is at the front of a band and must be able to perform and entertain.

the *other* guitarist

Two guitarists always seems like a good idea. It's not too difficult if one is pure rhythm and the other pure lead - no rivalry, no getting in each other's way. However, the best results come from having two good, versatile guitar players.

This is like clash of the titans for most bands but it need not be the case. If only you could talk and be objective about writing two guitar parts that always complemented one another. Well, you can dream - make sure it's not you that has the ego problem.

the keyboard player

Guitarists and Keyboard players usually get on OK. They've usually got the most knowledge - especially about keys and chords and are often the only member of the band that knows what is going on. Remember this when auditioning and need a bit of help.

the sax player

If you ask any sax player what style he plays they'll always say, in an affected husky, gin-soaked voice -

"Jazz, I play mainly jazz man".

Beware, this doesn't necessarily mean they can actually play jazz, or even know what it is - but they've learned that other musicians are impressed by this line and so use it all the time.

the drummer

What do you call the guy that hangs around with musicians? Yes, the drummer, the butt of most jokes.

Whilst it is true that your average drummer drinks to excess, smells like something between a brewery and a corpse and is generally the sort of person you'd cross the road to avoid, if he has the right priorities about his drumming you should accept his human failings gladly.

A drummer must be obsessed with playing TIME! Avoid drummers who don't know what a metronome is, or whose timing is clearly suspect.

If they spend the entire rehearsal practising ridiculous fills and tom tom rolls, yet can't keep the beat with accuracy and consistency - walk away, you don't need it.

the bass player

The other half of the rhythm section. What goes for drummers goes for bass players - if they can't play time and can't groove they should be buried at sea instead of making you look bad. Remember, when they dribble out of both sides of their mouths - you know the stage is level!

SHOWING OFF
THE ART OF PERFORMANCE!

the paying public

Whatever your ambition, there will come a time when you want to get out and perform live. It will help if you appreciate that you perform to entertain the public. If you're performing for yourself then there's something wrong.

Although this may sound obvious, the point is that good performance depends upon having the right attitude.

Whether an audience appears to be enjoying the gig or not, should not affect the way you and the band perform. Treat the audience with respect and play to them for their benefit. Also don't try and bully them into participation (especially if there are only a few people there propping up the bar).

Results will come if you project yourself to an audience and are obviously there for their enjoyment rather than some self-indulgence on your part.

eye to eye

Use your eyes to good effect when performing. Learn to look out to the audience, not at your instrument. Don't actually 'eyeball' anyone - pick 2 or 3 points on the back wall and focus on them. This gives the impression that you are playing to the audience.

It's worth practising the 'technique' of looking at points while you rehearse your guitar parts. If your eyes look confident, then even if you're nervous, you'll come across as a confident performer.

When soloing it can be better to look at the guitar. This has the effect of drawing attention to your hands and your playing - especially important if you're solo is spectacular.

The ultimate show-off is to look at the audience while soloing - if you can dart your tongue back and forth in a lurid manner then you're career as a rock 'n' roll legend is assured.

ALWAYS MOVE FORWARD TO THE FRONT OF THE STAGE WHEN TAKING A SOLO!

gigging

Keep the parts you intend to perform well within your limits. Gigs tend to throw up problems that you wouldn't believe. For example you may not be able to hear yourself, hear the vocals or even the drums. Things always go wrong with the equipment. This can usually be fixed, but you may have missed your chance to sound-check as a result. Panic may set in, or you may be rushed - all these pressures can take their toll, especially if your solos are over-ambitious.

Always take great care setting up your sound, make sure it works when the rest of the band are playing. Anyone can get a great sound at home with no other sound to affect your sound. In the sound check, get out in front - where the audience will be and listen to and tailor your sound from this position when the rest of the band are playing.

This may sound obvious now but get into the habit of collecting spares, picks (by the crateload), strings (at least 2 spare sets) leads (double up on everything if possible), keep all these together with a basic toolkit; screwdrivers, allen keys, solder and a soldering iron and ALWAYS carry them with you to rehearsals, studios and gigs.

Be aware of security! Never leave your valuable equipment unguarded for a second.

effects units

Very few guitarists can afford to ignore technology and effects. Distortion, reverb, delay, compression, phasing/flanging, chorus - the list of gadgets is endless. As I've said before, guitarists are judged on their sound almost above everything else this means you must understand what most effects are. You don't necessarily need to buy them all, choose carefully and buy sounds that fit your style of playing or fit the sound you imagine yourself playing soon.

recording

The best quick tip for recording is: BE PREPARED before you go into the studio. Studio time, at any level, is expensive. Know what sound you want, know your part thoroughly (eg. without vocals to guide you etc.). Get a good sound at source, before it goes to tape - never be fobbed off with a "we'll sort it out later in the mix", from the engineer.

Never stop if you make a mistake, you may interrupt the perfect drum take. Even if you do make a mistake, you can 'drop in' or go over the error later - so don't worry about the odd mistake. Having said that, the feel of a part or section is all about consistency and continuity, so it is preferable to record a line all the way through - at least aim to achieve this!

Are You Serious? Some Stuff to Keep You Going

the triplet - *dividing the beat into three*

Up till now you have only had to deal with (1) whole notes, (2) half notes (3) quarter notes and (4) eighth notes. The eighth notes meant; divide the beat into 2 equal parts. However, rhythm needs to be much more flexible than this. The beat can divide into 3 equal parts - triplets, 4 equal parts - sixteenth notes.

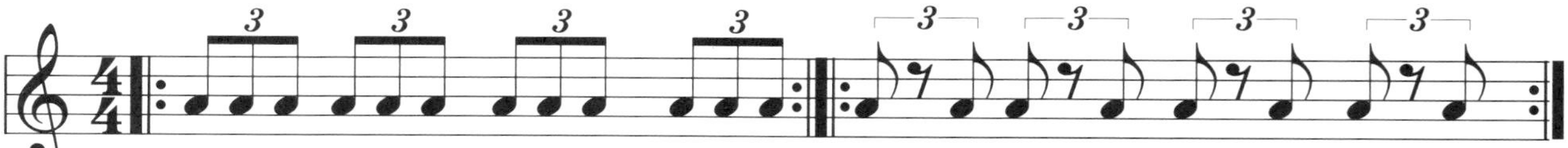

count: 1 & a 2 & a 3 & a 4 & a   1 & a 2 & a 3 & a 4 & a

count: 1 & a 2 & a 3 & a 4 & a   1 & a 2 & a 3 & a 4 & a

triplets and the blues

Now that you understand how to subdivide the beat into three, you will find it very easy to play a shuffle rhythm. Most blues is played as a shuffle - jazz also plays a similar feel but is known as swing.

Blues shuffle

muting and semi-muting

One of the simplest and most effective ways to modify the sound of the guitar is to mute or damp the strings. Generally this is done by the right hand; by tilting the hand slightly towards the bridge and gently damping the string(s). By varying the pressure, you can vary the degree of muting from full mute - where there is almost no pitch - only percussive sound, to a very subtle semi-mute, where the note sound is clear but the sustain is reduced. For rhythm playing, such as the example left (fig. 1), the mute is quite subtle - keeping the pitch and chords strong but improving rhythmic clarity.

fig. 1

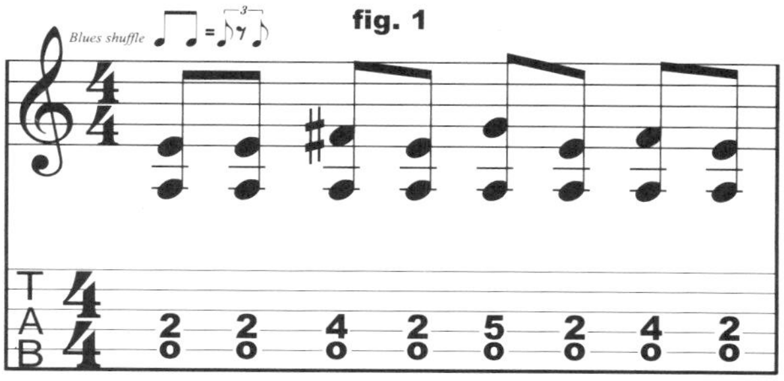

Use the pattern in fig. 1 to play a 12 bar blues. Fig. 1 represents the first bar - the 'A' chord. So (see page 21 if you can't remember the 12 bar progression) the pattern, as written, is repeated 4 times. Next, move the whole pattern to the D and G strings and play exactly the same riff. When it comes to the E chord, move to the E and A strings and play the riff - again in exactly the same way.

an introduction to 16th notes

Sixteenth notes greatly increase your rhythmic and musical potential. With this increase in creative possibility comes a considerable increase in difficulty.

When beginning to learn about sixteenth notes your first goal should be to understand how to divide the beat into four equal parts. Do this by counting;

1 - e - & - a, 2 - e - & - a, 3 - e - & - a, 4 - e - & a.

Practise the following exercises, which illustrate the most commonly used patterns.

When playing patterns or grooves that contain mixtures of sixteenth notes and other elements (eighth notes, quarter notes etc.) always keep the sixteenth note count (1 - e - & - a etc.) going. This will ensure that you play accurately and most important, will maintain the consistency of the groove.

fig. 1

muting with the left hand - *let's get funky!*

As well as damping the strings with the right hand, you can also mute with the left. All you have to do is release the pressure of the fingers on the fingerboard - but keep the fingers on the strings. Generally, this is either on or off because if the pressure is too light the open strings may 'break' through or you may get unwanted harmonics. The rhythm at fig. 2 is a good rhythm to practise - even without employing this technique. The note-heads marked 'x' are the percussive or muted notes. Try using a funky chord like the '9' chord shown - although any chord will do.

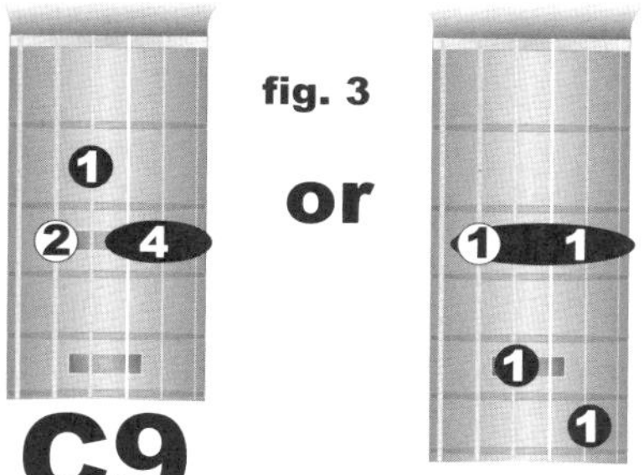

C9

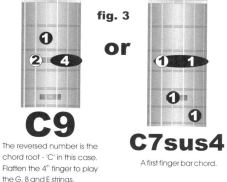

The reversed number is the chord root - 'C' in this case. Flatten the 4th finger to play the G, B and E strings.

C7sus4

A first finger bar chord.

string bending - *heart rending*

One of the most tempting and satisfying things to do on an electric guitar is to bend the strings. What matters technically, is that you can control the bend. The photo shows the best way to achieve a strong position on the neck for maximum control. It isn't essential to maintain this shape for every bend, simply that this is the strongest shape.

fig. 4

String bending provides the guitarist with a huge emotional weapon. By employing bends (tastefully) we can compete with vocalists and sax players on an emotional level. However, good taste is essential. You should always be trying to 'say' something when you bend a string. Usually, the effect is one of tension bending towards release. The longer you take to reach the point of release - the greater the tension effect. Good taste comes into it because you can overdo tension to the point where it becomes painful.

string bending exercise

fig. 1 fig. 2

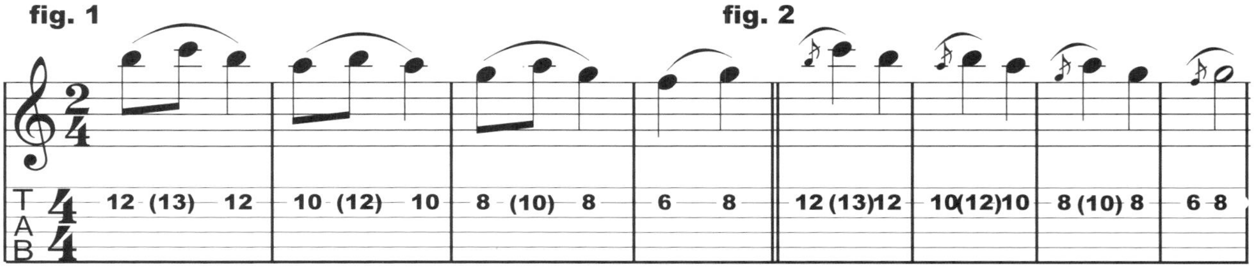

Fig. 1 is an exercise where the bend is quite slow and progressive. Slow bends are the hardest to time and control but are the most rewarding emotionally. Most bends are either semitone bends, as in the first two notes (B to C), or tone bends, such as A to B.

Fig. 2 plays the same notes as in Fig. 1 but this time the bend is very quick - the little note with a dash through it is used to indicate a note with no specific time value. So with this type of bend, you place you finger on the first note (indicated by the mini-note) and immediately bend to the main note.

You can also get into 'reverse' bends. These need to be 'planned' in advance, as well as requiring knowledge of exactly how much to bend, to reach a given note. With these bends you don't sound the bend up to a note, you bend silently and then pick the note and allow the bend to release - so the listener only hears the note bend down in pitch.

the 8 bar blues

Where there is more than one chord per bar the number of dashes indicate how many beats the chord lasts for.

| C | C7 | F | F♯° (//) A° (/) C° (/) | C (//) A (//) | D (//) G (//) | C (//) F (//) | C (//) G (//) |

a quick word on solo practise

This is not a book about the art of soloing. However, one thing you must get into is to record yourself playing chord progressions (preferably with a drum machine backing, or a metronome to keep time whilst you record). When you have an acceptable 'take' of your rhythm part, practise finding melodies. A simple way to get started is to play the scale that fits 'over' the chord first. This scale is found by playing from the root of the chord to its octave, in the key of the music. e.g. if the chord is Am and the music is in the key of C major, you play from A to octave A, using only natural notes - the key of C major.